Dec. 16, 97.

To Jack Kiser:
In appreciation of
our long and pleasant
relationship.
— Sarel Broodryk

The KRUGER NATIONAL PARK

WONDERS OF AN AFRICAN EDEN

The KRUGER NATIONAL PARK

WONDERS OF AN AFRICAN EDEN

NIGEL J DENNIS AND BOB SCHOLES

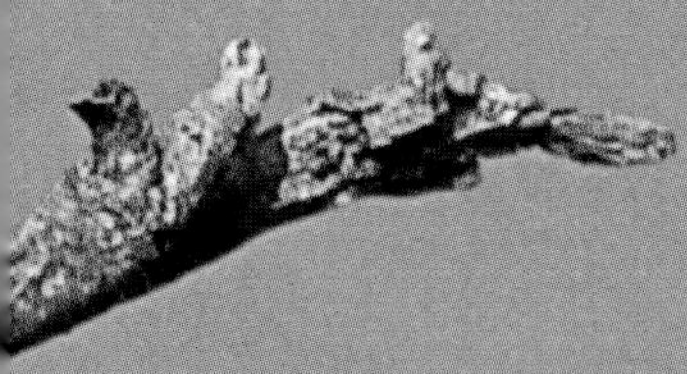

NEW HOLLAND

ACKNOWLEDGMENTS

I wish to thank the National Parks Board for its generous assistance and support during the two years I worked on this project. Special thanks to the following staff, researchers and friends: Keith Begg, Graham Cox, Andrew Deacon, Gert Erasmus, Willem Gertenbach, Johan van Graan, Jack Greeff, Salomon Joubert, Ben Lamprecht, Wayne and Inge Lotter, Marc and Sue McDonald, Menno Mennen, Sydney Miller, Gus Mills, Ian Milne, Flip and Annette Nel, Louis Olivier, Errol Pieterson, Ben Pretorius, Dr G A Robinson, Scott Ronaldson, Lynn van Rooyen, Bill and Sheila Ruysch, Schalk and Lorretha van der Sandt, Joep Stevens, Charl Steyn, Johan Steyn, Mark Taylor, Gert Viljoen, Ian and Merle Whyte, Tom Yssel and Gwin Zambatis.

My appreciation to Phil King and the staff at Citylab, Pietermaritzburg for their care in film processing, and to the ever-helpful staff of Photoworld, Pietermaritzburg. Although the great majority of photographs were taken specifically for this book, my thanks to Lesley Hay of ABPL, Sandton, Tim Harris of NHPA, England and John Kaprielian of Photo Researchers, New York for their assistance in allowing me to recall certain of my transparencies from earlier visits to the Kruger Park.

My sincere thanks to Bob Scholes for providing an engaging text and to the Struik staff, in particular Tracey Hawthorne, Eve Gracie, Alix Gracie, Ann Stapleton and Janice Evans, for their enthusiasm and commitment to the production of *The Kruger National Park: Wonders of an African Eden.* Lastly, a special word of gratitude to my wife Wendy for her companionship on all our numerous visits to the Park. Wendy's acute powers of observation resulted in many photo opportunities that I would otherwise have missed. I dedicate this book to her.

Nigel J Dennis
KwaZulu-Natal Midlands
February 1995

My thanks to the helpful staff at the Stevenson-Hamilton Library in Skukuza and to Nick Zambatis of the research staff for his careful review of the manuscript. The descriptions of the ecology of the Lowveld this book contains are seldom based exclusively on my own research, but originate from ideas generously shared by scientific colleagues over the years. A book of this nature does not lend itself to point-by-point acknowledgment in the text of my indebtedness to these individual sources even if I could remember them all; I hope that I have been able to present their ideas without distortion. My wife Mary has as always been a pillar of support. I dedicate this book to her.

Bob Scholes
Pretoria
February 1995

NEW HOLLAND

First published in 1995 by New Holland (Publishers) Ltd
London • Cape Town • Sydney • Singapore
Second impression 1996

ISBN 1-85368-593-3

New Holland (Publishers) Ltd
24 Nutford Place, London W1H 6DQ

Publishing Director: Tracey Hawthorne
Design Director: Janice Evans
Editor: Ann Stapleton
Designer: Alix Gracie
Cartographer: Steven Felmore
Consultant: Nick Zambatis
Reproduction: Hirt & Carter (Pty) Ltd
Printing and binding: Tien Wah Press (Pte) Ltd

HALF-TITLE PAGE: *Lion.* TITLE PAGE: *Bateleur.* OPPOSITE: *Kruger sunset.*
CONTENTS PAGE, LEFT: *Kudu;* RIGHT: *Tree squirrel.*

FOREWORD

No words man can drum up are adequate to describe the wonder of South Africa's Kruger National Park. What exactly attracts the more than 650 000 tourists, foreign and local, who visit the park each year? Is it only the 'big five', or does the magical attraction of the park really lie in the feelings it generates within its worshippers?

Over the years, the rivers, lifeblood of the park, have called animal and man alike to their banks; the undulating savannah, majestic baobabs and almost spook-like fever trees, the Lebombo mountains and the warm intimacy of a campfire on a sultry Lowveld evening, have lured back visitors time and again. Nigel Dennis's superb photography has managed to capture these many moods and faces of the Kruger National Park.

To single out characteristics would be impossible, as Kruger's makeup displays an intricate web of relationships and interactions. Nothing exists or happens in isolation. This is illustrated in Bob Scholes's text, dividing the park into seven ecological regions, for certain of which Kruger National Park addicts often show distinct preference, the topography and vegetation supporting the prevailing wildlife in each specific area.

In expressing my sincere appreciation and congratulating photographer Nigel Dennis and author Bob Scholes for producing a truly superb book on the biodiversity and magic of the park, I would also like to take the opportunity to thank Struik Publishers for, yet again, publishing not only a beautiful memento of any visit to the Kruger National Park, but also a book which will prove to be most informative to any reader.

The Kruger National Park has blossomed from its humble beginnings at the turn of the century into a world-renowned wildlife sanctuary and tourist attraction, now also sharing its expertise and benefits with neighbouring communities and opening its doors to the rest of Africa. It has become a haven, not only to the indigenous fauna and flora, but also for man. To quote Colonel James Stevenson-Hamilton, first warden of the park, our Cinderella has indeed become a princess.

Dr Robbie Robinson
Chief Executive
National Parks Board

Contents

INTRODUCTION

THE HISTORY AND BEGINNINGS OF THE KRUGER PARK

The Kruger National Park is no longer merely a national asset. It is part of a dwindling global treasure, the collective natural heritage of all mankind.

The vast interior plateau of Africa is known in South Africa as the 'Highveld'. Its edge is marked by the great escarpment which, in the corner where South Africa, Zimbabwe and Mozambique intersect, is separated from the Indian Ocean by a broad plain known as the 'Lowveld'. This is the setting for one of the great conservation areas of the world, the Kruger National Park.

A considerable mythology has arisen around the origins of the Kruger National Park in which President Paul Kruger of the *Zuid-Afrikaansche Republiek* (ZAR) far-sightedly set aside this vast area that future generations might know Africa in its original state. In fact, his role in creating the reserve was only one in many[5, 20]. The Kruger Park was not the first conservation area in Africa, or even in South Africa. For many years it had been apparent that wildlife, which formed a hidden foundation of the Boer republic's

ABOVE: *Young chacma baboon.* LEFT: *Lazy lion.* RIGHT: *Egyptian Geese keep a watchful eye on a young crocodile. Crocodiles frequently catch unwary birds.*

LEFT: *A wild dog near Shingwedzi in the mopane-covered country of the northern part of the Kruger National Park.* RIGHT: *An alert female waterbuck on the watch for predators.*

economy, was dwindling. The *Volksraad,* the governing body of the ZAR, had empowered its executive to declare areas of state land closed to hunters. The purpose of such regulations was not conservation as we now understand it (the protection of nature for its intrinsic value) but to provide a 'game reserve' where wildlife could breed so that it could later be shot.

By 1889 the decline of the great herds was almost complete. In 1894, after several years of procrastinating, the *Volksraad* proclaimed the Pongola Reserve, adjacent to the southern border of Swaziland. Various private citizens, sport-hunting associations and public officials continued to press for a reserve in the Eastern Transvaal, however. This lobbying eventually culminated in the proposal to protect an area between the Crocodile and Sabie rivers. The *Volksraad* records show that the first formal proposal was made in 1895 by J L van Wijk, the representative from Krugersdorp, and the member for Barberton, R K Loveday, and was nearly unanimously approved.

It was three years before the necessary regulations were published by President Paul Kruger: the proclamation of a 'government reserve' appeared in the *Government Gazette* of 26 March 1898. The fledgling reserve became known as the Sabi Game Reserve.

This precursor of the Kruger Park occupied an area of approximately 250 000 hectares, which included the present-day Skukuza, Malelane and Pretoriuskop restcamps. The first custodians of the Sabi Reserve were two policemen: Sergeant Izak Holzhausen, who was based in Nelspruit, and Corporal Paul Bestbier, based in Komatipoort. The effective control of the reserve was interrupted between 1899 and 1902 by the war between the British Empire and the Boer republics.

Major James Stevenson-Hamilton, intelligence officer in the Sixth Inniskilling Dragoons, was appointed warden after the war. This turned out to be an inspired choice. Stevenson-Hamilton was descended from a long line of land-holding gentry, steeped in the tradition of game stewardship. His devotion to the survival and furtherance of the new reserve bordered on an obsession.

When Stevenson-Hamilton arrived in the Lowveld in 1902 he found very little wildlife in the area that he had been sent to protect. He immediately began to curb poaching, to the amazement and annoyance of the local white and black inhabitants.

In 1903 he lobbied successfully to have the boundary of the reserve extended 20 kilometres to the west. In the same year the colonial administration created the Shingwedzi Game Reserve in the northern part of the Lowveld. This reserve comprised an area of 500 000 hectares, between the Limpopo and Letaba rivers. James Stevenson-Hamilton was to be in charge of both reserves.

The area between the Sabi and Shingwedzi reserves had been surveyed as private farms. Most of these were owned by large land companies but were only nominally occupied by them. Stevenson-Hamilton was able to negotiate a leasing scheme, reviewed every few years, whereby the private farmland effectively became part of the Sabi Reserve. Stevenson-Hamilton thereby gained control of what was to become, decades later, the greater Lowveld conservation region.

His uncompromising opposition to hunting in the reserves earned him respect but few friends. When the lease agreement for the area west of the present Pretoriuskop Restcamp expired in 1912 he was forced to allow the area to be used as winter grazing for sheep.

In 1914 Stevenson-Hamilton rejoined the British Army in France for the duration of the First World War. During his absence the Union government appointed a commission to deliberate on the future of the reserves. Since game hunting was no longer a mainstay of the economy in South Africa, the idea of the game reserves had lost its original purpose and there was considerable pressure to make the area available for farming. With the decline of hunting as an economic activity, the main reason for the creation of the reserves disappeared. They were expensive to maintain, generated no revenues, occupied land that could be used for other purposes and harboured dangerous beasts. Pressure mounted to have them deproclaimed, as were other reserves, including the Pongola, during this period. The legal status of reserves rested on a single regulation that could be reversed by administrative whim.

The survival of the Sabi and Shingwedzi reserves was achieved by harnessing them to a new, radical idea: the national park. National parks, as they were conceived at the beginning of the twentieth century, had an aesthetic

RIGHT: *The baobab is a timeless symbol of the arid regions of Africa. This magnificent specimen was photographed during late afternoon in the far north of the Park.*
FAR RIGHT, TOP, MIDDLE AND BOTTOM: *The characteristic fishing technique of the Yellowbilled Stork involves shading the water with one wing. Fish that are attracted into the shadow created by the wing are quickly snapped up.*

rather than economic justification. This idea excited the imagination of the South African public, already well on the path to an urban and industrial future. Stevenson-Hamilton, impressed by the success of national parks in the United States of America, lobbied for a more permanent status for the Lowveld reserves. The commission eventually recommended that the reserves be given the status of a national park, but no action was taken.

Many years of uncertainty followed, and the fortunes of the reserves reached a low ebb in 1922 when pressures from farmers, mining houses and land companies seriously threatened their existence. Stevenson-Hamilton continued to lobby for a national park, however, with the support of a number of prominent citizens and state officials. The Minister of Lands, Colonel Deneys Reitz, was won over but soon thereafter was swept from power when a new government was ushered in by the rising tide of Afrikaaner nationalism. It was fortunate that the new Minister of Lands, Piet Grobler, grand-nephew of Paul Kruger, also favoured the creation of a national park and championed the legislation in parliament. It was at this stage that the name 'Kruger National Park' was suggested. The bill was seconded by the leader of the opposition, General Jan Smuts, and was passed with acclamation.

On 31 May 1926 the National Parks Act was promulgated with the Kruger National Park as its first protected area. Counting from the proclamation of the Sabi Reserve in 1898, the Kruger National Park is the second oldest formally-conserved area in Africa and at nearly two million hectares, one of the largest.

The area proclaimed as the Kruger National Park was made up of certain parts of the Sabi Reserve (the area which now incorporates the

Sabi-Sand, Timbavati and Klaserie private nature reserves was excised), and the Shingwedzi Reserve, as well as the privately owned farms and state land between them. There have been some minor boundary adjustments since that time, but the basic form of the Kruger National Park has remained the same.

Since 1926, the Park has become an important national institution. For instance, when the threat of coal mining in the northern portion of Kruger arose in the late 1970s, shared concern for the Park was revealed as one of the few issues able to unite an increasingly divided white population of South Africans. The petition against the proposed mining gathered a record number of signatures, thereby causing the plan to be shelved.

Following the transition to democracy in South Africa in 1994, the Park once again faces political challenges. A new conservation debate is just beginning, with the Kruger Park at its heated centre. How can this national asset best be used for the benefit of all South Africans, including those yet to be born?

There are unresolved issues of ownership: were the original inhabitants of the area that has become the Kruger National Park unjustly dispossessed of their land? If they left willingly, were they adequately compensated?

The conservation of biological diversity seems an abstract luxury to their descendants, many of whom live in the crowded tribal lands that border the Park. The tall grass, abundant firewood and plump game represent an underused resource to them. To the thousands of black Africans outside the fences, the Kruger National Park's facilities seem designed to cater exclusively for wealthy white people and foreigners, while the needs of the black citizens are ignored. They ask: 'Can animals be more important than people?'

The Kruger National Park will rise to these challenges, as it has risen to challenges in the past, because the merits of its existence are robust. The way in which it serves both the needs of the people and those of nature will undoubtedly change in the future, in response to an evolving understanding of those needs. This is as it should be.

OPPOSITE: *Buffalo share many characteristics with domestic cattle, including susceptibility to the same diseases and the vagaries of the Lowveld climate. This herd was found near Letaba during the dry season – note the dust kicked up by their hooves.* ABOVE: *A restful scene with impala grazing below a sycamore fig tree in the Shingwedzi River valley.* BELOW: *A female Melba Finch.*

COLONEL JAMES STEVENSON-HAMILTON

James Stevenson-Hamilton[20, 28] was a Scottish cavalry officer who fought in the South African War. When peace was declared, he was offered the task of turning the legal abstraction of the Sabi Game Reserve into an on-the-ground reality; and made it his life's work.

He was a small man but boundlessly energetic and with a dogged streak which would see the fledgling reserves through the many uncertain times leading up to the proclamation of the Kruger National Park.

Reading between the lines, Stevenson-Hamilton must have been a hard and uncompromising taskmaster. The vigour with which he stamped out poaching in the new reserve earned him the nickname 'Skukuza', meaning 'the one who turns things upside down' (Skukuza camp was named for him). Not all of the men who applied for positions as game rangers met his high expectations or shared his work ethic, military sense of discipline and unassailable integrity. He was also dismissive of people who had achieved their understanding of nature through academic study, rather than in the hard school of the bush.

In later years, Stevenson-Hamilton had the vision and the ability to steer his 'Cinderella' from its origin as a game reserve to a more secure position as a national park.

If any single person is to be credited with creating the Kruger National Park as we know it today, that person should be Colonel James Stevenson-Hamilton.

He longed to serve the Kruger National Park until his last gasp – 'to die in harness', as he put it. This was not to be and he retired as warden in 1946, after having held the position for 44 years. Stevenson-Hamilton died in 1957 at the age of ninety on his farm near White River. His ashes and those of his wife, Hilda, were scattered on the Shirimantanga koppie where a commemorative plaque has been placed on this favourite lookout of his, 12 kilometres south of Skukuza. Colonel James Stevenson-Hamilton will forever be a part of the Kruger National Park, the wildlife sanctuary that he fought so hard to make a reality.

Lowveld Landscapes

An Overview

This is a story of connections:

the invisible links between organism and

environment that make up the fabric

of a working ecosystem.

The essential difference between a national park and other institutions devoted to conserving biological diversity is that national parks preserve not only the plants and animals, but also the processes that allow them to survive and adapt to a changing environment. In other words, the central purpose of national parks is to conserve ecosystems rather than species. Genetic conservation could be achieved in a test-tube, yet instinctively we know that there is more to life than that. The whole is more than the sum of the parts; the difference is the essence of the science of ecology. A frustration encountered by the nature-loving public is that there are few guides that help them understand and visualize the web of interactions and relationships that make up the ecosystem. This book attempts to address that problem. In this respect it differs in intention from the many fine books written about

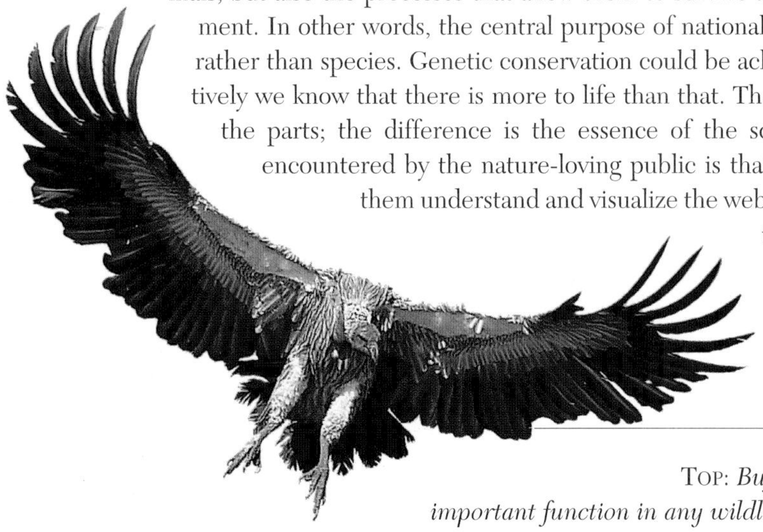

Top: *Buffalo.* Left: *Vultures perform an important function in any wildlife area. These scavengers play a sanitizing role in that they clean up carcasses which would otherwise become infested with the maggot larvae of blowflies.* Opposite: *Dusk in the Kruger National Park.*

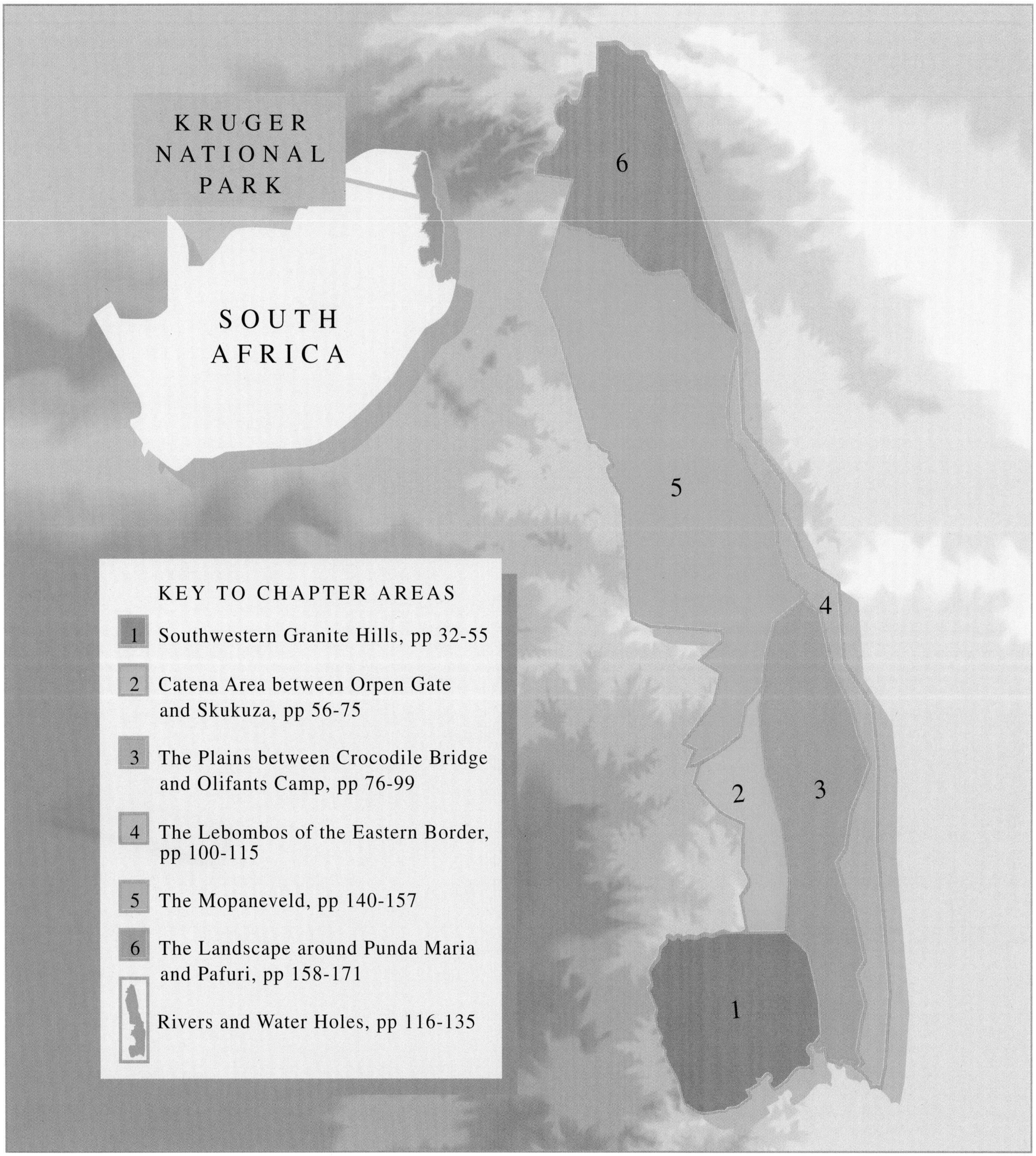
KRUGER
NATIONAL
PARK
SOUTH
AFRICA
6
5
4
2
3
1
KEY TO CHAPTER AREAS
1 Southwestern Granite Hills, pp 32-55
2 Catena Area between Orpen Gate and Skukuza, pp 56-75
3 The Plains between Crocodile Bridge and Olifants Camp, pp 76-99
4 The Lebombos of the Eastern Border, pp 100-115
5 The Mopaneveld, pp 140-157
6 The Landscape around Punda Maria and Pafuri, pp 158-171
Rivers and Water Holes, pp 116-135

the individual parts of the ecosystem, which in this case are the plants, animals, insects, birds and reptiles of the Kruger National Park.

In order to perceive these connections, we need to adopt a different way of seeing. We are often, quite literally, not able to see the wood for the trees; metaphorically, we need to put aside our binoculars and magnifying glasses and float above the earth as if in a balloon. We need to look at the landscape in its entirety rather than just at its parts.

RIGHT: *The white rhino cow generally allows her calf to walk slightly in front of her, perhaps because her rearward vision is poor.*
BELOW: *Accommodation offered in the Park consists of cool and comfortable thatched huts or two- and three-bedroomed cottages such as this one in the Bateleur Bushveld Camp. Campsites for tents and caravans are also provided at most of the main camps.*

ABOVE: *Hippos spend most of the day submerged in water; they are able to hold their breath for up to six minutes. At night these mammals emerge from the rivers to graze. Hippos are responsible for maintaining the close-cropped lawns which fringe many Lowveld rivers.*

Ecologists use the word 'landscape' in a particular sense. To them it refers to the combination of climate, soil, topography, vegetation and animals that forms an interacting unit – the tangible manifestation of the abstract concept of 'ecosystem'. A landscape is usually large enough to include several distinct plant communities and many different types of soils. The unifying factor is that the same pattern of relationships between the climate, soil, topography, vegetation and animals is repeated in a predictable way throughout the landscape. The threads that bind it together and give it form are ecological processes; the ebbs and flows of energy, matter and genes are the currency of nature's economy.

Landscapes have spatial dimensions and the dimension of time. In landscapes, just as in the construction of a sentence or a work of art, the position of the parts in relation to one another is crucial to understanding how they connect. Often *where* an organism is to be found is a vital clue as to *why* it is to be found there. The time dimension is less obvious because it is invisible but it is equally essential to our understanding. Everything we see in the landscape has a history, like a legion of shadowy ghosts marching behind it.

A logical place to begin describing the landscapes of the Lowveld is with the breakup of the supercontinent of Gondwanaland, nearly 200 million years ago. That ancient upheaval created Africa and mapped the pathway along which the African landscapes were to evolve. Unlike other continents, Africa did not move off over the ocean, passing through different climatic zones and crunching into other landmasses. It only drifted slightly farther north and the climate and land-forming processes in Africa have therefore been remarkably free of major cataclysms for at least 100 million years; this has allowed the evolution and maintenance of an unusually diverse fauna and flora, intricately adapted to each other and to their environment.

Just as the shape and height of a building are determined by its foundations, so does the soil set the limits of form and function of terrestrial ecosystems. Plants are constructed mainly of carbon, hydrogen and oxygen, elements that are drawn from the atmosphere by harnessing the energy of sunlight. Soil is the source and store of all the other elements that plants require in order to build their varied forms. The differences we observe in the structure of plant communities are due mainly to differences in the climate and the soil. The successive

LEFT: *The genetic makeup of all cheetahs is virtually identical. The world population must have been reduced to a handful of individuals at some time many thousands of years ago. This would have led to a reduced gene pool and eventually to a similarity of genes once the population recovered.* ABOVE: *Newborn giraffe are concealed in the bushes for a few days until they are steady enough to keep up with their elders.*

ecological layers of plants, herbivores and carnivores can only be as abundant as the supply of nutrients permits. Similarly, the soil can only be as rich as the rock from which it is formed. Geology is therefore a good place to start to understand the landscape.

The skeleton of the major continents comprises great rafts of rock in the broad geological family known as granitoids. These rocks are the oldest part of the Earth's crust and are appropriately called the Basement Series since they are the foundation of the terrestrial world.

Granitoids are acidic, igneous, crystalline rocks. They consist mainly of the relatively light elements silicon and aluminium, neither of which is needed in significant quantities by most plants and animals. Soils formed from granites are therefore relatively infertile. Much of the silicon is in the form of quartz, which is

hard and slow to weather. Granite landscapes are therefore hilly and sandy.[2]

Sometimes the granitic rafts split, and the underlying magma wells to the surface in the form of volcanoes and lava flows. These fall mainly into a second broad geological category, the basic igneous rocks. They are much richer

LEFT: *Cape Glossy Starlings are common birds in restcamps throughout the Park. They are omnivorous and eat mainly insects and fruit. The Greater Blue-eared Starling is similar in appearance but has violet-coloured flanks and blue, mainly unglossed ear coverts.*
OPPOSITE, TOP: *Playful sparring between the young of chacma baboons will later develop into the more aggressive displays observed between adult males.*

LEFT: *Night drives, guided by members of the Park staff, depart shortly before sunset from the major restcamps. These tours provide the best opportunity for visitors to observe the abundant night life of the bush, especially since it is against Park regulations for unaccompanied visitors to be outside the camp gates after dark. The night drives last for two or three hours and are conducted in open vehicles (a warm jacket is therefore essential). Take along a pair of good binoculars – you will find them as useful at night as they are in the daytime, since binoculars slightly amplify the illumination provided by the guide's spotlight.*

in the elements which plants need and therefore produce fertile soils. They weather more rapidly than the acid igneous rocks do, leading to flat and clayey landscapes.

A third rock family, the sedimentary rocks, is formed from the solidification of debris resulting from the weathering of other rocks. Their soils vary in fertility, depending on the richness of the original material that produced the sediment. The final category, also with fertility intermediate between the acid and basic igneous rocks, is the metamorphic rocks. They are formed from other rock types by the application of pressure, heat and chemicals.

The geology of the Lowveld is organised into broad bands, oriented in an approximately north-south direction[24]. The bands represent successive layers, once horizontal but now tilted downward towards the east by the immense forces that were associated with the shifting of the continents. So, a journey from east to west across the Park is also a trip backwards in time, from a mere 50 million years ago to the beginning of the world.

A belt of granitoids extends from the base of the escarpment in the west to approximately midway across the Park. These form the gently rolling landscapes of the southern and western

TABLE 1

The number of species found in the Kruger Park in relation to the total number of species in southern Africa (the area south of the Zambezi and Cunene rivers), Africa and the world.

GROUP	KRUGER	SOUTHERN AFRICA	AFRICA	THE WORLD
Mammals	147	227	843	3 927
Birds°	492	718	1 655	8 981
Reptiles^	118	285	1 010	6 214
Amphibia†	34	84	610	3 900
Freshwater fishes	49	270	42 700	?
Trees and Shrubs	404	1 500	?	?
Grasses	224	847	?	9 700
Other Plants	1 275	22 000	?	250 000

° *(breeding and non-breeding)*
^ *(snakes, lizards, terrapins, tortoises, crocodiles)*
† *(frogs and toads)*

parts. The granites were covered by layers of sediments and then capped by a layer of lava, known collectively as the Karoo Sequence[4]. The rocks of the Karoo Sequence are more erodible than the ancient granite to the west and the younger rhyolite to the east, and form the broad, flat, central plain of the Park.

The oldest members of the Karoo Sequence are shales and mudstones, sedimentary rocks originating from the fertile alluvium of lakes and deltas and therefore producing fertile soils themselves. Some of these layers contain coal and fossil plants, evidence of a luxuriant vegetation in the distant past. Overlaying the shales are sandstones derived from wind-borne quartz particles. The sandstones weather to form porous and infertile sands. The youngest element of the Karoo Sequence is basalt, a basic lava that welled up from the deep fissures formed at the time of the Gondwanaland disintegration, blanketing the land surface. The basalt forms the fertile, black, clayey soils of the plains immediately west of the Lebombos.

The Lebombo hills (the word means 'ridge' in Zulu) stretch from Shingwedzi in the northern part of the Kruger Park, southwards for 500 kilometres to KwaZulu-Natal, marking the eastern border of the Park. They are formed of rhyolite, an acid igneous rock which weathers very slowly and produces a shallow, stony soil.

ABOVE: *Giraffe drinking at a water hole with zebra in the background.*
LEFT: *The two full turns of this kudu's horns show that it is about three years old and sexually mature. The birds are oxpeckers which are scouring the kudu's hide for parasites.*
OPPOSITE, ABOVE: *A young waterbuck concealed from predators in the grass.*
OPPOSITE, BELOW: *The Blackheaded Oriole can easily be identified by its liquid, melodious call.*

Sills of gabbro, a basic igneous rock related to basalt, coil like a giant python across the southwestern Kruger Park. A sill is a more-or-less horizontal intrusion between the strata of a pre-existing geological sequence. In this case the intrusion occurred not long before the breakup of Gondwanaland, into overlapping conical stress fractures caused by the buildup of subterranean pressure. The contrast between the

fertile but arid gabbro-derived soils and the surrounding soils derived from granite is dramatic and abrupt, and is reflected in the differences in vegetation and animals. A good place to see this transition is on the road between Skukuza and Pretoriuskop, near Shitlhave Dam.

An intrusion of hard gabbro forms a ruler-straight line of hills ('rykoppies') between Bushbuckridge and Skukuza; it is easily identified from the air as one approaches the runway at Skukuza. This is a dyke rather than a sill, since it intruded vertically rather than horizontally, through several pre-existing strata.

After the geology and landform, climate is the next major factor that determines the ecological potential of a landscape. The climate of the Lowveld generally follows a trend from wetter and cooler weather in the south and west to drier and hotter in the areas of the north and east[11]. These trends cut across the geological belts previously described, and the resulting range of combinations of climate and geology is the main source of the great variety in the vegetation and wildlife of the Lowveld.

The hot, rainy season lasts from about November to April, the warm (generally frost-free), almost rainless season from May to October. This predictable alternation of wet and dry is essential to the existence of savanna or bushveld, which consists of a mixture of trees and grasses in proportions that vary between places and times.

Like other semi-arid regions of the world, the Lowveld is exposed to great variations in the amount of rainfall received in any one year. The reason for the low rainfall in the Lowveld and its large variability lie in the position of the region relative to the main weather-generating circulation systems. The latitude of the Park coincides with a zone of dry, descending air. This results in lots of sunshine and warm temperatures but little rain. It is only when the tropical circulations shift southwards in the summer months that the high-pressure cells can be elbowed aside, sucking in moist air from over the ocean and sometimes leading to spectacular thunderstorms.

The third element that defines a landscape

is the plants and animals contained in it. The diversity of life in the Park is illustrated by the numbers of species listed in Table 1 on page 23 – about what would be expected per unit area of land for a tropical, semi-arid region. The total number of species in the Park is greater than exists in many whole countries, but Kruger is bigger than many countries. The relatively small fraction of the South African flora conserved in Kruger is simply a reflection of the enormously rich plant diversity in the country.

The final element that determines the form and function of a landscape is also part of the animal life but is such a special and influential species that it deserves a category of its own: it is Man, the self-conscious primate. We tend to think of the pre-colonial landscape as being free of the influence of human disturbance but this is not so. The obvious impacts of large-scale agriculture and urbanization in the Lowveld appeared only this century but the more subtle influence of millennia of hunter-gatherers and several centuries of pastoralists have nevertheless left their imprints on the landscape.

The human population of the Lowveld at the time of the proclamation was probably at its lowest historical point. The human economy depended on cattle and wildlife; the Lowveld was rife with nagana, a fatal disease of cattle carried by the tsetse fly. The region had not always been infested with tsetse fly; it appears to have been absent in 1725 when the Dutch

ABOVE: *Lions are not as lazy as they may appear: most of their activity takes place at night.*
RIGHT: *Visitors can while away the hot midday hours by spending some time bird-watching or game-spotting from a hide. Pictured here is the hide at the Bateleur Bush Camp. It is situated at a water hole and affords many excellent viewing opportunities. When making use of a hide, one should respect the other visitors' need for peace and silence by remaining absolutely quiet.*

RIGHT: *Ground Hornbills are omnivorous. Here one makes a meal of a puff adder, one of the few venomous snakes found in the Kruger National Park. These large birds are a threatened species in South Africa, and the Lowveld has become their main refuge.*
BELOW: *This male waterbuck clearly shows the forward-swept horns that are characteristic of these antelope.*

explorer De Kuiper visited. The wildlife decimation initiated by hunting was completed by rinderpest, a virulent disease of cattle and wildlife that originated in Asia and swept through eastern and southern Africa between 1896 and 1898, killing about 95 per cent of the cattle and related antelope species, such as buffalo, in the areas affected by the disease. An ironic consequence of the rinderpest epidemic was that it freed the Lowveld of tsetse fly. The development of effective prophylactics against malaria in the 1930s, combined with liberal use of newfangled insecticides, such as DDT, to combat mosquitoes, was the final step that opened up the Lowveld for human development.

The twentieth century has seen the Lowveld transformed from an inhospitable wilderness into a region of high human population and significant economic activity. Most of the land occupied by the Kruger Park is too arid or infertile to support crop agriculture and its value as a tourism venue exceeds the income that could be expected from cattle ranching. The Park has become the core of a vast natural resource management area that includes privately and communally owned protected areas, as well as reserves in the adjacent countries. Tourism may soon become a mainspring of the southern African economies and the wheel will have turned full circle: once again the welfare of the people will depend on the variety and abundance of the African landscape.

The state of the landscape in pre-colonial times is of more than purely academic interest: it is one factor that is considered when trying to decide what the landscape should look like now. For many years the ecological management of the Kruger Park was based on the premise of keeping it in its 'natural state', which was defined as its condition prior to the disturbances of the late nineteenth century.

TOP AND BOTTOM LEFT: *Wild dogs are the most threatened of all the large predators in the Park. They require home ranges of several hundred square kilometres and have a reputation for being wanton killers of livestock. This does not make them popular with farmers: one of the reasons why they are unlikely to be found outside protected areas.*
OPPOSITE: *Mating in lions may be initiated by either member of the pair.*

This raised some practical problems, since our knowledge of the Lowveld at that time is limited. There are few photographs, and the early descriptions are vague and untrustworthy. Conditions around the time of proclamation were possibly quite unnatural due to rinderpest and hunting. Even if the desired state were perfectly known, our grasp of ecological processes is still inadequate to allow landscapes to be steered unerringly towards a given target. And what if the target has moved: should we keep on aiming at the place where we think it used to be?

The idea of the 'balance of nature' has been quietly abandoned by most professional ecologists. The overwhelming evidence is that nature is almost never in balance, at least not at the small scales and over the short periods to which we are accustomed. In the past, when conservation managers intervened to redress some perceived imbalance, they usually ended up making things worse. Instead of trying to keep ecosystems in a particular state, conservationists now try to keep the processes driving the shifting states as unimpeded as possible.

General Visitor Information

There are several flights a day between the Skukuza landing strip and Johannesburg International Airport near Johannesburg. The Park may be entered by motor vehicles at any one of eight gates; but visitors must take note that the gates to the Kruger National Park and its restcamps are open only during daylight hours. Visitors are not permitted to enter the Park unless they have sufficient time in which to reach their accommodation without exceeding the speed limits, which are 50 kilometres an hour on the surfaced roads and 40 kilometres an hour on the gravel roads, before the gates close. Visitors who arrive at their camps after the gates have closed may be fined.

Vehicles must have a solid roof, and visitors are not allowed to leave their vehicles except in the restcamps and at designated places. Visitors may drive on any road in the Park except those marked with a no-entry sign. (Hire cars and guided tours are available.)

Accommodation consists of a range of huts, cottages and tents of different sizes and degrees of luxury. Visitors may pitch their tents or park caravans in the campsites located in most restcamps, or may use the permanent 'safari' tents.

Accommodation may be booked by writing to or telephoning the National Parks Board in Pretoria: PO Box 787, Pretoria 0001 (fax: (012) 343-0905, tel: (012) 343-1991); or in Cape Town: PO Box 7400, Roggebaai 8016 (fax: (021) 24-6212, tel: (021) 22-2816).

Popular camps become booked up very rapidly at peak times, but midweek accommodation is usually available at fairly short notice if you are willing to be flexible about the camps in which you stay. Day visitors do not need reservations except over the busiest long-weekends when the number of cars entering the Park is restricted to 5 000.

Basic groceries, alcoholic and non-alcoholic drinks, clothing and souvenirs are available from shops in the restcamps. Most restcamps have a restaurant where breakfasts, lunches and suppers are served, and drinks and snacks are available in-between times.

Credit cards are accepted in all camps (except for payment of fuel purchases). Petrol is available at all camps and at the entrance gates. Only a few of the Park's camps have public telephones, but all of them have emergency telecommunication facilities.

The Kruger National Park is flanked by several privately owned wildlife areas which offer luxurious accommodation and personalized attention. Within a one-hour drive of the Park, visitors will also find numerous hotels, campsites and lodgings that range from the luxurious to the very basic.

It is essential to take anti-malaria pills before entering the Kruger Park and to use insect repellent at night, especially between the months of October and May. Inform your doctor that you have been in a malaria area if you develop flu-like symptoms within three months of returning home.

Types of Restcamp

There are four basic types of restcamp in the Kruger Park: main camps, private camps, bushveld camps and camping-only camps.

All except Olifants, Orpen and Mopani offer thatched huts and campsites, in approximately equal proportions. Main camps have restaurants which are open for breakfast, lunch and supper (exceptions are Orpen and Crocodile Bridge, which are small camps located at gates), shops at which basic groceries (including beer and wine), books and curios can be purchased, petrol stations and laundromats. Most have facilities for day visitors, though Lower Sabie is an exception. Some have public telephones, swimming pools, in-camp nature trails and educational displays. The main camps are: Berg-en-Dal, Crocodile Bridge, Letaba, Mopani, Olifants, Lower Sabie, Pretoriuskop, Punda Maria, Satara, Shingwedzi and Skukuza. Some have luxury houses available to private visitors when not in use by their (mainly corporate) sponsors.

Bushveld camps are a more recent development aimed at diversifying the range of options available to visitors. The idea is to offer a more exclusive atmosphere, while remaining affordable. Bushveld camps are considerably smaller than main camps, ranging from 32 to 80 beds. The roads leading to them are for the exclusive use of the residents of the camp, which helps to preserve the atmosphere of peace and quiet. Accommodation is essentially the same as that in the main camps, but there are no restaurants and shops. The cost is a little higher than for the main camps, but the reservation procedure is the same. There are six bushveld camps in the Kruger Park: Bateleur, Jakkalsbessie, Biyamiti, Shimuweni, Sirheni and Talamati.

Private camps must be reserved in their entirety by a single party. They accommodate 12 to 19 people in huts, cottages and houses. The party staying there may be smaller than the total number of beds, but the price is based on the camp as a whole. If fully occupied, it is as inexpensive as staying in a main camp. The principle advantage is that the camps are small, quiet and completely occupied by your group. There are no visitor facilities other than the accommodation itself. There are five private camps: Jock of the Bushveld, Boulders, Malelane, Roodewal and Nwanetsi.

Campsites are for the exclusive use of visitors with their own tents or caravans. They offer levelled sites, which may be occupied by up to six persons each. Some of the sites are grassed but many are bare earth; most have at least some shade. There are communal bathrooms, kitchens and washing-up areas, which are sufficient in number and immaculately maintained. Most main camps offer campsites as well as standard accommodation. In addition, Maroela Campsite is exclusively for campers, while Balule Campsite has only three six-bedded huts.

The Kruger Park also offers wilderness trails: Boesman, Metsimetsi, Napi, Nyala Land, Olifants, Sweni and Wolhuter. Participants are accommodated in trails camps.

Opposite: *This magnificent tusker is enjoying a comfortable browse. Note how it uses its trunk to feed. Males have an evenly sloping forehead while females have a sharper angle between the forehead and the top of the head.* Below: *The giraffe is at its most vulnerable when it is drinking and does so with obvious nervousness. A series of valves in the blood vessels of the neck prevent a sudden rush of blood to the brain.*

Gate Opening and Closing Times

	Open	Close
JAN	05:00, 05:30*	18:30
FEB	05:30	18:30
MAR	05:30	18:00
APR	06:00	17:30
MAY-AUG	06:30	17:30
SEPT	06:00	18:00
OCT	05:30	18:00
NOV-DEC	04:30, 05:30*	18:30

* Entry Gates only

BONES OF THE EARTH

THE LANDSCAPE OF THE SOUTHWESTERN GRANITE HILLS

Rolling hills, often crowned by a huge granite dome or a pile of massive, balanced boulders, characterize the southwestern part of the Kruger National Park, the landscape of which is built on granite.

Solid granite weathers along the lines of weakness created by veins of feldspar, leaving behind heaps of balanced, blocky boulders. The granite domes form by repeated heating and cooling and the penetration of water that causes layer after layer of rock to peel off over a period of thousands of years. The koppies, with their many fissures and crannies, are ideal habitat for klipspringers, baboons and leopards. The warm stone slabs are also a good place to spot lizards and, if you are very lucky, a python.

When granite weathers, it leaves behind a coarse quartz sand and produces a fine clay. Over a period of thousands of years rainfall washes the clay down into the valleys, resulting in clayey soil which supports small-leaved, thorny *Acacia* trees and more palatable ('sweet') grasses. The ridge tops have sandy, infertile soils, supporting large-leaved, thornless trees,

TOP: *White rhino.* LEFT: *Most visitors to Kruger will have spotted the vibrant colours of the Lilacbreasted Roller.* OPPOSITE: *A granite hill, known as a 'koppie' in Afrikaans, covered here with a fringe of fig trees.*

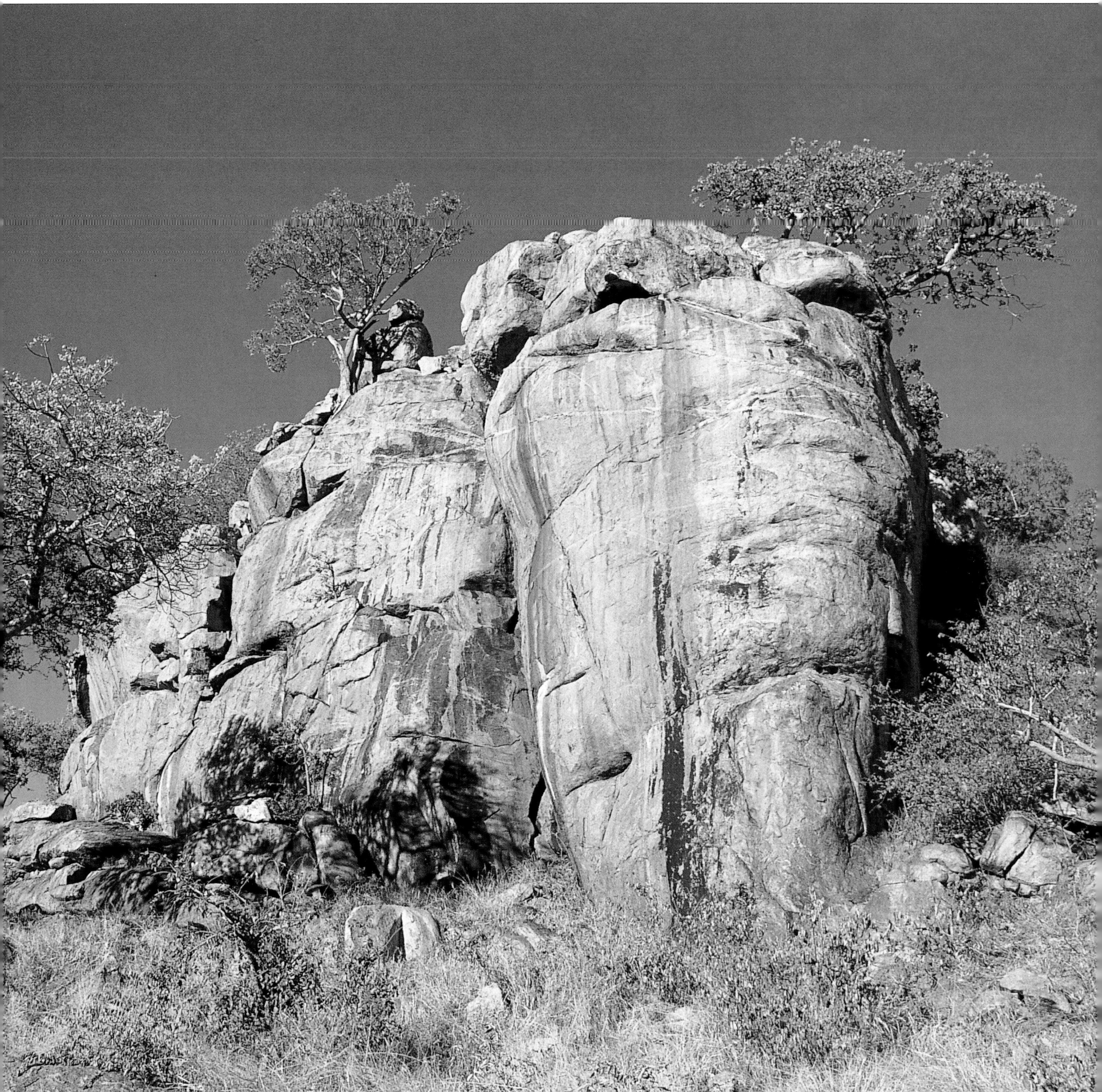

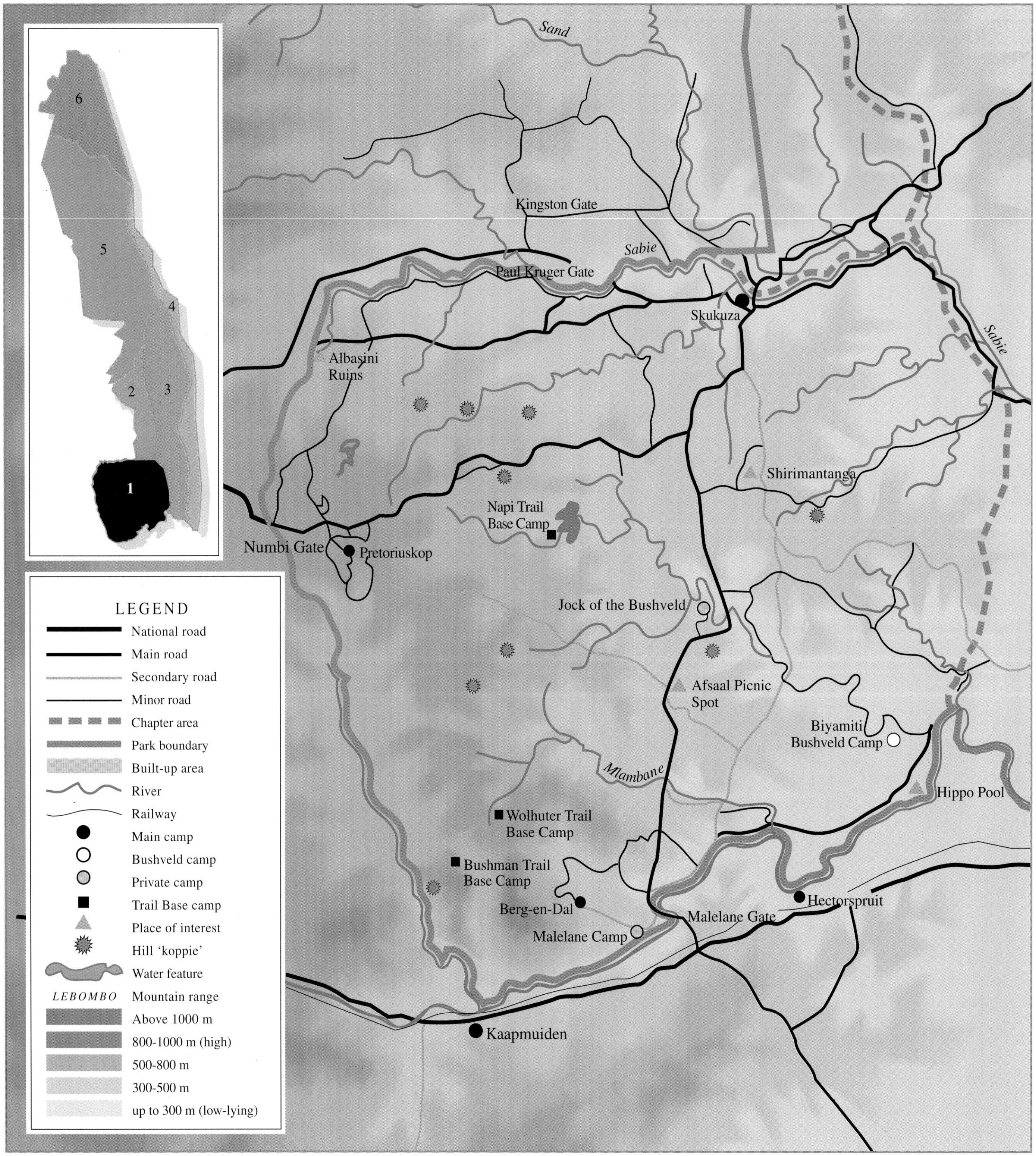
6
5
4
3
2
1
LEGEND
National road
Main road
Secondary road
Minor road
Chapter area
Park boundary
Built-up area
River
Railway
Main camp
Bushveld camp
Private camp
Trail Base camp
Place of interest
Hill 'koppie'
Water feature
LEBOMBO Mountain range
Above 1000 m
800-1000 m (high)
500-800 m
300-500 m
up to 300 m (low-lying)
Sand
Kingston Gate
Sabie
Paul Kruger Gate
Skukuza
Sabie
Albasini Ruins
Shirimantanga
Napi Trail Base Camp
Numbi Gate
Pretoriuskop
Jock of the Bushveld
Afsaal Picnic Spot
Biyamiti Bushveld Camp
Mlambane
Hippo Pool
Wolhuter Trail Base Camp
Bushman Trail Base Camp
Berg-en-Dal
Hectorspruit
Malelane Gate
Malelane Camp
Kaapmuiden

such as the raasblaar (*Combretum zeyheri*), and a cover of tall but unpalatable ('sour') grass. The total number and density of animals is higher in the more fertile valleys but interesting species, such as sable antelope and mountain reedbuck, are more likely to be spotted on the ridges.

The division of the landscape into these two vegetation types is a microcosm of the savanna pattern of the whole of Africa. The central plateau of Africa is known to geomorphologists as the African erosion surface. It supports broad-leaved savannas, while the more recent erosional surfaces around its edges and in the deep valley basins support fine-leaved savannas.

The African erosion surface is over 30 million years old, and is usually underlain by the acidic, crystalline rocks of the African Shield (such as the granitoid rocks found in the southwestern part of the Park). The soils would not have been very fertile to begin with and have become progressively poorer over the millennia as rain leached out the nutrients. Because they are higher in elevation than more recent erosion surfaces, they are wetter and cooler. The younger erosion surfaces, on the other hand, are often formed on sedimentary rocks, or on basic lavas which welled up as a consequence of the splitting of Gondwanaland. Their soils, while arid, tend to be fertile.

The easiest way to tell broad-leaved savannas apart from fine-leaved savannas is to look for thorns. If most of the trees in an area are conspicuously thorny, you are looking at a fine-leaved savanna. Chances are, the leaflets will be tiny (only a few millimetres long) and compound, and the tree will belong to the Subfamily Mimosoideae of the legume family. The best-known and most widespread genus in

ABOVE: *Giraffe are not deterred by thorns but their rate of feeding is reduced to a level tolerable to the plant. The thorns embedded in the thick mucous covering of the tongue are gradually shed as it is replaced by new cells.*
RIGHT: *Vervet monkeys are mostly vegetarian but they will not pass up an opportunity to snatch a passing insect, raid weavers' nests for eggs, or exploit the contents of visitors' huts.*

RIGHT: *The jakkalsbessie or ntoma tree (*Diospyros mespiliformis*) is a stately member of the ebony family and is often found growing along river banks or on termite mounds. Its Afrikaans name refers to the fact that jackals have sometimes been seen eating its fruits. The wood is pinkish-brown when first cut but turns black as it dries. It was once widely used in the Lowveld. The foliage, usually a glossy dark green, is a translucent golden-red when the leaves are young. The dense canopy is usually alive with birds, especially when the fruit, which is edible but not very tasty to humans, is ripe.*

RAASBLAAR

Combretum zeyheri, *the raasblaar, is a typical broad-leaved savanna tree from the sourveld hill country of the southwestern regions of the Kruger National Park. The four-winged seed-pod is characteristic of the genus* Combretum, *but in the case of* C. zeyheri *it is unusually large.*

The dry leaves and fruits make a rustling sound in the wind, giving rise to the Afrikaans common name, which means 'noisy leaf'.

this Subfamily is *Acacia*. Broad-leaved savanna trees, in contrast, are thornless, have simple leaves several centimetres long, and belong mainly to the Combretaceae Family or the Subfamily Ceasalpinioideae of the Fabaceae.

The presence or absence of thorns reflects the different ways in which these two groups of trees protect themselves. The main consumers of tree leaf in broad-leaved savannas are insects, especially their caterpillar larvae. Thorns offer little protection against them, but hairy leaves and digestion-inhibiting chemicals are very effective. Up to one third of the mass of the leaf may consist of a class of chemicals known as tannins. Tannins bind to proteins and cellulose, preventing the digestive enzymes from attacking them, and since enzymes are proteins themselves, the tannins deactivate them. Animals soon learn to avoid plants with a tannin content higher than about five per cent. As a result, typically less than a tenth of the leaves in broad-leaved savannas are eaten by browsers.

A much higher fraction (a third to a half) of the leaves in fertile savannas are browsed. The building of tannins is probably too 'expensive' in terms of the carbon that must be invested, and would prevent the plants from spending it on other structures. Their growth rate on fertile soils is not limited by nutrient supply. It is 'cheaper' for them to replace the leaves they lose to browsers than to defend them heavily. These plants defend themselves with thorns, which are relatively cheap to produce, and a

type of tannin which can rapidly be synthesized when needed. Thorns do not prevent browsing – watch a giraffe or a kudu eat from a thorny branch. Thorns merely slow down the rate of consumption to a level the plant can tolerate.

The highest point in the Kruger Park is Khandizwe, 15 kilometres west of Malelane, at 839 metres above sea level. The relatively plentiful rainfall here (up to 900 millimetres a year) often results in an abundance of tall grass. This grass is palatable when it is young but during

ABOVE: *The boulder-strewn koppies of the granite hills are favoured by leopards as safe places to raise their cubs. There are many caves and crevices between the towering blocks of granite. Baboons overnight on the rocky crags and often fall prey to the leopards.* LEFT: *The tips of the branches of the naboom or candelabra tree (*Euphorbia ingens*) are lined with the fleshy flowers. These trees can grow to up to ten metres in height.*

LEFT: *Klipspringers are confined to rocky habitats. Their hooves are cup-shaped, rubbery and almost circular, providing them with sure-footed agility as they bound from boulder to boulder. Their first reaction on being disturbed is to stand absolutely still.*
OPPOSITE: *The Brownhooded Kingfisher is one of several kingfishers in the Kruger Park not associated with rivers.*

the late summer and the winter dry season the protein content of the leaves drops steadily. Eventually it falls below the level necessary to sustain the digestive bacteria in the guts of grazers. Grazers can literally starve to death while surrounded by a sea of grass. The southwestern corner of the Park is the main area of 'sourveld'.

Wild grazers survive in sourveld in two ways. They seek out those parts of the landscape that have more nutrients and are therefore less sour. In the Pretoriuskop landscape this means concentrating in the valley bottoms. The second method of adaptation concerns the grazer metabolism. A large-bodied grazer such as a buffalo can extract more nutrition from low-quality forage than a small-bodied grazer can. This is because the larger the body, the longer the time the food remains in the gut. Antelope and bovids (which include buffalo and cattle)

Termite Mounds

Large termite mounds are restricted to upslope margins of the vleis in this area. Higher up there is insufficient clay for building, and lower down they become flooded. The mounds are about 100 metres apart because termites are fiercely territorial.

When the mound is young (colonies can persist for centuries), a seed may be dropped on it and grow into a tree. The tree attracts birds and more seeds are dropped. Soon the mound is covered by a miniature forest of mostly fruit-bearing, bird-dispersed trees, which are a favourite habitat of the Green Pigeon.

are ruminants, having a large, four-chambered stomach in which the fermentation process that breaks down cellulose takes place. The forage passes sequentially through each stomach, being held in each for a certain period of time. This is a very efficient process but it proceeds at a fixed, slow pace. The horse family, including zebra, have evolved a different type of digestive system in which the fermentation takes place in the large intestine rather than in the stomach. This is less efficient than the four-chambered stomach but is more tolerant of poor-quality forage since the rate at which food is processed can be increased in times of stress.

Elephants combine a large body with a hindgut fermentation system. Their gut is so large that they can swallow twigs and strips of bark. This material is hardly digested at all but because it is always available and a large amount can be processed, elephants can survive long periods when little grass, their preferred food, is available. It is easy to see when they are under dietary stress because the proportion of woody material in their dung increases.

Where the valleys are not too steep, the combination of clay accumulation and high rainfall leads to the formation of a marshy grassland in the valley floor known as a 'vlei' (or *dambo* farther north). The soil in the vlei is not continuously wet but for several months every few years it is completely saturated – a condition savanna trees cannot tolerate, so the vleis are treeless. Ecologists refer to grasslands formed by water as hydromorphic grasslands. These habitats are scarce within the Park and support particular species of animals and birds.

LEFT: *The Yellowthroated Longclaw particularly favours the long grass of vleis.* ABOVE: *The Black Stork is one of the rarer storks in South Africa. It is always found alone or in pairs. Black Stork nests are often associated with colonies of Cape Vultures, leading to speculation that they use the circling vultures as guides to thermals.* FAR RIGHT: *Yellowbilled Hornbills nest in holes in trees – the females are sealed into the hole until after the eggs hatch, with only the beak sticking out. She and the fledglings are fed by the male. Hornbills can often be seen circling and diving for insects over veldfires.*

Although the soils of the vleis are relatively fertile, the excess water causes grasses there to grow tall and fibrous. Most game will not eat this grass except under drought conditions. It is the preferred habitat, however, of the reedbuck. Most of the reedbuck in Kruger (at least 400, and probably more, since they are hard to count) are found in the Pretoriuskop-Malelane area. Listen for their distinctive alarm whistle.

Another species that favours vleis is the oribi, a small antelope similar in appearance to a duiker. The oribi is relatively rare in South Africa but is quite widespread in central Africa. The pioneers of the late nineteenth century reportedly hunted oribi in the Pretoriuskop region. By the early twentieth century they were extinct. Beginning in 1969, repeated efforts were made to reintroduce oribi to the Park. Of the 145 released only a small number survive. The Kruger Park must have been at the extreme limit of oribi distribution last century,

when climatic conditions may have been a little wetter than at present. It has been concluded that the Park no longer affords suitable habitat for oribi and reintroductions have ceased.

When the vleis are burned, they become a magnet for all species of game. The residual water in the soil, even in the dry season, causes fresh, green, highly palatable grass to emerge soon after a fire. The short grass and absence of trees allow the herds to see predators at a distance, giving them time to escape.

The area west of the Nsikazi River, the present western boundary of the Park, was part of the Sabi Reserve between 1903 and 1923. It was held under a lease arrangement, and from 1912 onwards the entire Pretoriuskop area was used as winter grazing for sheep. The practice at that time was to burn the grass every year in autumn, to provide fresh feed in winter. The informed opinion was that excessive burning was the main cause of the declining condition of South African rangelands, so once the Park was established in 1926 this practice stopped. Fires were actively excluded until 1954.

The consequence was a dramatic increase in the density of the bush around Pretoriuskop. Early photographs of the Pretoriuskop area show a predominantly grassy landscape with occasional trees. Today it is a wooded landscape except for the vleis. This may have contributed to the changes in animal populations between the turn of the century and the present.

The early 1950s marked the beginning of the scientific management of the Park. For the first time biologists were appointed to management positions. When burning was re-instituted they laid out a series of fire experiments. Each fire trial consisted of 13 five-hectare patches, separated from each other by firebreaks. One patch was never burned, and in most cases has become a dense woodland. The other patches were burned once every three years. Findings have confirmed that fire is crucial to maintain the balance of trees to grass. Occasional burning also removes the old, dead grass which prevents sunlight from reaching the new leaves.

Until recently, the Park was burned in large blocks, nominally once every three years. The ultimate decision to burn a plot was based on an assessment of how much moribund grass had accumulated and how much other forage was available for grazers[31].

When deliberate burning is undertaken, a strip of grass is ignited along the downwind side of the block to be burned. When it has burned a sufficient distance into the block, the fire-fighting team moves to the upwind side and ignites a strip there. The flame front formed by this upwind ignition sweeps very rapidly across the block until it meets and is extinguished by the previously lit 'backburn'.

Since 1993 a less rigid system has been adopted in keeping with the Park's mission to manage

the environment with as little interference in natural processes as possible. When a fire breaks out, a ranger assesses whether it was started by natural causes (principally lightning) or ignited by humans. If evidence suggests the former, the fire is monitored for research purposes and rangers ensure that facilities in its path are protected by firebreaks. If it appears that people lit the fire, no effort is spared to extinguish it.

It seems amazing that any animals could survive a line of fire that sweeps across the landscape, but they do. There are cases of animals being trapped and killed but these are relatively rare. The antelope of the African plains have evolved with fire as a condition of their environment: when they sense one approaching they move from its path. Smaller animals such as rodents and reptiles generally shelter below ground, where temperatures hardly rise at all.

Insects, too, have evolved responses to fire. When ticks, waiting on plant stalks for host animals, detect the increase in carbon monoxide in the air heralding an approaching fire, they abandon their perches and burrow into the ground. Grasshoppers flee in swarms ahead of the flames, providing a feast for wheeling squadrons of hornbills, shrikes, kites and storks.

Birds such as the Wattled Plover rely on the bare, blackened areas for nesting sites. Their eggs are speckled with black, and are almost invisible against the ash and charred grass. The parent birds can see approaching nest-raiders, such as jackals, from a great distance, and fly up to harass and distract them.

Geophytes are a category of plants that live predominantly underground. Their roots are large, fleshy bulbs or tubers. The water and energy stored in the bulb allow geophytes to send up a flowering stalk before leaves are produced, often during the dry season, immediately after a fire. As the only flowers present at such times, they attract the full attention of the pollenators. Leaves are then produced and the stored energy is recharged before the surrounding grasses begin to block the sunlight.

ABOVE: *Every kudu has a unique pattern of stripes and facial spots which allows biologists to follow the lives of individuals. A bull spends several years as a bachelor before it can successfully challenge a dominant male and gain access to the female herd. Once dominant, the life expectancy of the male drops due to the stress of maintaining its position. Stephenson-Hamilton described the kudu as the 'acme of Nature's efforts to attain perfection of type'.*

BABOONS

*The chacma baboon (*Papio ursinus*) is the only baboon species found in the southern African subregion and is mostly confined to that region (records of yellow baboons require confirmation). Chacma baboons belong to the Subfamily Cercopithecinae, the members of which all have human-like shapes.*

These baboons are highly gregarious, living in troops of up to 100 animals, although 50 would be more average.

Order is maintained in the troop by a continuous interplay of social interactions, from grooming and playing through to outright aggression.

There are nearly 200 troops of baboons in the Kruger National Park, each with a fairly distinct home range. A troop of baboons will cover up to 15 kilometres during a single day's foraging. They forage for insects, bulbs, fruits and fleshy stems, among many other things: it has been said that it is easier to list the items not eaten by these omnivores than what they do eat! Their nights are spent on ledges of rocky outcrops or in large trees.

LEFT: *The flowers of the common coral tree* (Erythrina lysistemon) *are a glorious sight in the late dry season and the seeds have long been collected by the children of Africa as 'lucky beads'.* OPPOSITE: *Male impalas that have not successfully gathered a breeding herd form bachelor herds.*
OPPOSITE, BELOW: *Tawny Eagles are common in the major game reserves but scarce elsewhere in southern Africa.*

Grasses also take advantage of the fact that the temperature near the ground surface hardly rises during a fire. Unlike most woody plants, which have their growing buds at the tip of their branches, grass buds are located at the base of the plant, at ground level. Here they are protected from both fire damage and grazing. The grass plant extracts most of the nutrients from leaves as they die and stores them for future use.

Fire kills grass tufts if it is very hot and burning close to the ground, into the wind. The buds and young leaves are vulnerable during early summer when they have just begun to grow.

Mature savanna trees are almost immune to fire. The most sensitive parts are the leaf buds and the cambium (the thin layer of cells that lies immediately below the bark and is responsible for the production of wood on its inner side and bark on its outer side). If the temperature of either rises above 60° C for more than a few minutes, they die and further growth is impossible. The cambium is protected by the bark, which is corky, flame resistant and an excellent insulator. The leaf buds are mostly above the flame zone and are protected by enclosing scales. Buds within the flame zone are killed and the tree must produce new buds from the cambium. This is why you may see trees with dead branches but new leaves sprouting directly from the bark. A particularly intense fire will kill the above-ground cambium and the tree must resprout from below the ground.

Fire controls tree height and the diameter of trees rather than the number of trees per hectare. Many of the grasslands of the Kruger Park are full of small trees which may be quite old but are prevented from escaping the flame zone by repeated fires that burn them down to ground level each time. If fires do not occur for five or ten years, these saplings grow taller than the flame zone and can then no longer be controlled by fire. This is why the Pretoriuskop landscape is now stuck in a woodland state.

Fire is also instrumental in the eventual death of the trees, in a roundabout way. The bark of most savanna trees is damaged at some stage during their life. Frequent causes are porcupines gnawing at the base of the tree or an elephant stripping the bark. The scar of such a wound seldom heals over completely and the small patch of exposed, dead wood becomes a target for wood-boring beetles, which in turn introduce dry-rot fungi. When a fire next occurs, this dead patch burns, creating a small hollow. Over the years the hollow grows larger and larger. Many old savanna trees are completely hollowed out on one side, usually the side that is downwind during the fire season. Eventually the tree will be blown over or it will be pushed over by an elephant. The whole process, from the porcupine's first nibble to the moment the gnarled and hollowed bushveld giant crashes to the ground, may take up to a century. Even then the tree does not necessarily die – it often resprouts from the stump.

There are factors besides fire that are also involved in determining the tree-grass balance. Most of these other factors work in concert with fire. For instance, where browsers are common, these animals prune the young trees and prevent them from growing out of the flame zone. The tree-cover tends to be denser on the koppies than on the plains, mainly because the rocky slopes of these hills are partially protected from fire. There is also an overall control that is applied by the interaction of climate and soil. As rainfall increases, so does the height and density of trees. Furthermore, with equal rainfall, there tend to be more trees on sandy soils than on clayey soils.

OPPOSITE: *A young hyaena developing its jaw muscles on a fragment of bone. Hyaenas are highly cooperative hunters and breeders. Members of the clan assist each other in bringing food for the cubs. The laugh of the hyaena is one of the unforgettable sounds of a wilderness experience in the Kruger National Park.*
ABOVE: *Male lions are hunters while they are nomadic bachelors, but should they succeed in gaining a pride, they tend to leave the bulk of the hunting to the lionesses. Their weight can reach up to 240 kilograms and is of assistance in the bringing down of some of their larger prey animals, such as mature buffalo.*

Savannas pose a bit of a problem for ecologists. There is an axiom in ecology that 'complete competitors cannot coexist'; in other words, where two populations of organisms use exactly the same resources, one would be expected do so slightly more efficiently than the other and therefore come to dominate in the long term. In temperate parts of the world, either trees dominate (as in forests) or grasses dominate (in grasslands). Yet, in savannas grasses and trees coexist.

The classic explanation proposes that trees have deep roots while grasses have shallow roots. The two plant types are therefore able to coexist because they are not in fact competitors: the trees increase in wetter climates and on sandier soils because more water is able to penetrate to the deep roots. Trees do indeed have a few small roots which penetrate to great depth, but most of their roots are in the top half-metre of the soil, just where the grass roots are.

Under the Lowveld climate very little rainwater ever penetrates below one metre into the soil. The water table in most of the Kruger Park area is fifty or more metres deep. It is only rarely recharged by rainfall and then gets only about one per cent of the total rainfall. Trees in general clearly could not rely on that source as their only supply of water, although some species do. The trees that have access to the deep water table are known as phreatophytes, and can easily be recognized in the dry season because they are covered in green leaves while the other species are bare. The nyala berry (*Xanthocercis zambeziaca*) and the rain tree (*Lonchocarpus capassa*) are good examples of phreatophytes found in the Park. Before the days of sophisticated geophysical surveys, boreholes were often located by drilling them close to these water-indicating trees.

Trees are able to store a little water and energy from one season to the next and are therefore able to produce leaves very rapidly at the beginning of the growing season. Unless a drought occurred in the previous year, the trees will be flush with leaves even before the first rains occur. Grasses, on the other hand, must grow their new leaves using the current year's rainfall and energy, and this takes several weeks. Trees therefore have an opportunity at the beginning of each season to grow with very little competition from grasses for either water or nutrients, and in fact this is when they do most of their growing. They usually get another chance for exclusive use of the resources at the end of the season when the grasses begin to die back after flowering. It is the grasses that are generally at a disadvantage; so why do savannas not all become woodlands?

Ecologists now view savannas not as 'equilibrium systems' but as 'disequilibrium systems', where the trees will come to dominate if they get a chance. They are generally prevented from doing so by repeated disturbances – fire or large herbivores, for instance. Disturbance is now widely accepted as being an integral and essential part of ecosystem function. Even disturbances caused by humans are no longer automatically considered 'unnatural'.

The higher rainfall and cooler climate of the southwestern corner of the Kruger Park made it a favoured settlement area for people ever since the Stone Age. The numerous caves and overhangs were used by Bushmen, or the San people, who probably coexisted with Bantu people in the area until a few hundred years ago. Keenly observed and gracefully executed San paintings are found in overhangs on many of the koppies (take the three-day Bushman guided walking trail). These are one source of information on the prehistorical animal diversity in the area: it was partly on the strength of a painting in the Pretoriuskop region, with the distinctive horns and hump of a Lichtenstein's hartebeest, that this rare species was reintroduced to the Kruger National Park in the 1980s.

What were once village sites of Bantu-speaking people can easily be located on aerial photographs of the region as little islands of high fertility in the sea of sourveld. Some of these village sites date from the Iron Age, up to 800 years ago. Their inhabitants were pastoralists

Grey Lourie

The stridently nasal alarm call of this bird has given it the common name of 'Go-away Bird'. They are predominantly fruit-eaters that are usually seen in pairs or small groups, often perching in the upper branches of trees. They are the dowdy bushveld cousins of the brilliantly coloured Purplecrested Louries that occur in the riverine forests and are often seen in the river-side camps of the Kruger National Park.

The Grey Lourie has a long tail and crest, and is one of the most obvious birds to be found in the bushveld. It is completely grey and usually very vocal and conspicuous. However, when breeding, the Grey Lourie is more furtive and will slip away from the nest when a potential predator is still quite a distance away. Although it prefers dry woodland savannas (both broad-leaved and fine-leaved), this ash-grey bird is dependent on water and has to drink regularly. Like the Knysna and Purplecrested Louries, this bird has a habit of leaping and bounding from one branch to another. It also runs along the branches like a mousebird.

LEFT: *The orange colour and the long floral tube of the aloe flower signal that sunbirds are the main pollinator. Here a bumblebee lends a hand.*

and crop farmers who protected their cattle at night by herding them into a kraal made of thorn branches in the centre of the village. The accumulation of nutrients in the manure of the animals persists as a patch of nutritious grass.

White explorers, traders and hunters appeared regularly in the Pretoriuskop region from the middle of the nineteenth century. The ill-fated Trichardt party of Voortrekkers trekked through the present-day Kruger Park in 1838 on their way to Delagoa Bay in what was then Portuguese East Africa. Half the party died of malaria after they had reached their destination. The only adult male survivor was Karel Trichardt, son of the party leader. In 1845 he returned to blaze the first official wagon trail through the region, connecting Ohrigstad to the coast. It was little used until after the discovery of gold at Pilgrim's Rest on the escarpment west of the Kruger Park. The preferred route of transport riders on their way to Delagoa Bay was through the Pretoriuskop hills.

One of the transport riders was Percy FitzPatrick, who later became a mining magnate and political leader on the Witwatersrand. He is best remembered for the book he wrote

ABOVE: *Elephants are able to swallow strips of bark and even twigs, which allows these animals to survive long periods when little grass is available to them. When grass is available it makes up about three-quarters of the diet. Elephants pluck grass by curling the end of the trunk around the stems. Like most herbivores, their diet is limited less by the availability of carbohydrates than by proteins, minerals and vitamins. Elephants will therefore spend a disproportionate amount of time delicately picking off seedpods and fruits, also with the sensitive tips of their trunks.*

entitled *Jock of the Bushveld*. Many of the incidents he described can be linked to locations in the Pretoriuskop vicinity and are commemorated with brass plaques illustrating his fearless and indefatigable terrier, Jock. To this day, terriers are the preferred companions of rangers in the Lowveld.

The management of the Kruger National Park has a policy of reintroducing those species of animals which are known to have existed in the area during the period of historical record. One of the mammal species that temporarily disappeared from the Lowveld, around 1896, was the white rhino. Following its rescue from the brink of extinction, through the efforts of the Natal Parks Board, six were re-established in the Pretoriuskop region in 1961. The population in the Kruger Park has now reached approximately 1 800 animals, spread throughout the Park and adjacent reserves. The total world population of white rhino now numbers about 7 000 and is steadily increasing.

The Africa-wide outlook for the black rhino is less hopeful. Once far more common and widespread than the white rhino, demand for rhino horn has resulted in a dramatic decline in its numbers and a steadily shrinking distribution. Black rhino disappeared from the Lowveld

LEFT: *Sable antelope are likely to be spotted on the ridges of the granite hills. The Kruger Park is the southern limit of their distribution.*
RIGHT: *The white rhino population in the Park now numbers about 1 800.*
BELOW: *There are over a hundred species of dung-associated beetles in the Park. One group of them, in the scarab family, is well known for rolling the dung into compact balls, which are buried after an egg has been laid in the centre.*

around 1936. Twenty animals were reintroduced to the Pretoriuskop area in 1971 and have increased in number. This is now an important and relatively secure population numbering more than 200, and perhaps as many as 470; since black rhino favour dense bush they are very difficult to census accurately. However, each rhino can be individually identified from the scars it bears and, in order to detect poaching, detailed records are kept of nearly every rhino in the Lowveld.

The rhino species are a good example of what ecologists call 'niche separation'. The niche of an organism can be thought of as its occupation: how does it go about making its living? According to the competitive exclusion principle, if two species have exactly the same niche, then the better competitor must, in time, eliminate the weaker competitor. Although they look quite similar and are closely related, the two rhino species occupy such different niches that they hardly compete at all. The white rhino is a grazer. That is why it holds its head low, and has a broad, square mouth, hence its other name, the square-lipped rhino. The black rhino is almost exclusively a browser. It therefore holds its head high, and has a beak-like lip which gives rise to its alternative common name, the hook-lipped rhino. The dung of the black rhino is easily differentiated from that of the white rhino by the number of short twig fragments it contains, the ends of which are neatly clipped at a 60-degree angle, as if by pruning shears. The molars of the black rhino are able to slice through twigs up to one centimetre in diameter. Elephant dung also frequently contains twigs, but these are in longer pieces, with shredded ends.

The habitat preferences of the two rhino species are also different. White rhino favour savannas or grasslands. Their large bodies allow them to eat relatively coarse grasses, although

ABOVE: *The large-spotted genet is mainly nocturnal, lying up under cover during the day. They are excellent climbers although much of their foraging is done on the ground. The diet consists of mice, insects, spiders, small birds, frogs, toads and reptiles.*
RIGHT: *A female waterbuck. Only male waterbuck carry horns. The male will rub its face and the base of the horns against the female's back when initiating copulation. If the female is receptive, the male will rest its head on the female's back or tap her between the hind legs with its fore legs. Copulation may then follow.*

they prefer shorter, sweeter grasses. Black rhino favour dense thickets of *Acacia* bushes, which are usually found in the valleys.

In some cases the evidence for the previous occurrence of a species within the Park is inferred from what is known about the habitat requirements of the species; mountain reedbuck and grey rhebuck have been reintroduced on this basis. They are found elsewhere in South Africa in hilly grassland areas which receive relatively high annual rainfall. Only the southwestern corner of the Park satisfies these conditions, and may have represented the margins of the prehistorical distributions of these animals. Despite reintroductions these antelope species are still rare within the park.

The Bateleur was once widespread in South Africa but is now restricted to the Lowveld. It is common in the skies above the Pretoriuskop region, and you may be lucky enough to see it performing aerial acrobatics ('bateleur' is French for 'juggler'). Although it is a bird of prey it obtains a large part of its diet from carrion, especially while young.

It differs in aerodynamic design from most other large raptors, having almost no tail and a head which protrudes far in front of the wings. This design adapts the Bateleur for highly manoeuvreable, low-altitude cruising, which usually makes it the first bird to arrive at a carcass. The disappearance of the Bateleur from much of the Transvaal has been attributed to the decline in the number of carcasses as cattle ranching replaced game, and especially to the poisoning of carcasses by farmers intending to kill nuisance animals such as jackals. With increased conservation awareness among farmers, this attractive bird may reclaim its former habitat.

A combination of the rinderpest outbreak of 1896 and the use of cattle dips containing arsenic led to the extinction of the Yellowbilled Oxpecker within South Africa by 1904. In the mid-seventies, Yellowbilled Oxpeckers were once again seen in the northern part of the Kruger Park. Within fifteen years, they had penetrated all the way to Malelane, recolonizing the habitat which they once occupied. The game populations in the Kruger Park (and especially buffalo, which are the favoured host) had recovered sufficiently to support a viable oxpecker population. The bush war in the southeast of Zimbabwe had caused a suspension of cattle dipping in the area of land that separated a remnant population of these birds from the northern Kruger Park, and they were able to migrate across it. Less toxic anti-tick poisons have subsequently been developed for use on cattle, so it is anticipated that the Yellowbilled Oxpecker will continue its march southwards, eventually regaining its former territory inside and outside of reserves[14].

Tourist Facilities in the Southwestern Kruger Park

Skukuza is the headquarters of the Kruger Park administration and is the largest camp, with a bank, library, telephones, doctor and police station. There are beds for 634 visitors and camping facilities for a further 480.

Pretoriuskop, eight kilometres from Numbi Gate, is a good camp for a summer visit because it is relatively cool and has a large, shallow swimming pool ideal for children. Accommodation consists of 344 beds and campsites for 240 people. Berg-en-Dal is one of the few camps with conference facilities and it also has an attractive swimming pool. This is another good summer choice, and nine kilometres from Malelane Gate. There are 356 beds and campsites for 420 visitors.

Malelane is a private camp which has 19 beds. As a private camp it must be booked *en bloc*. It is one kilometre from Malelane Gate. Jock of the Bushveld is also a private camp, accommodating 12 people.

Biyamiti is a bushveld camp with minimal facilities, built in rustic style. The 22-kilometre road leading to the camp winds down the delightful Biyamiti River and is for the exclusive use of the 70 residents, all of whom are accommodated in huts and cottages.

The Bushman, Wolhuter and Napi walking trails all operate in the hilly, roadless wilderness of the southwestern Park. Each of these trails is

highly recommended: the Bushman and Wolhuter trails for their scenery and interesting plant life, and Napi for its game.

Afsaal picnic spot is almost halfway between Skukuza and Malelane. It provides hot water for beverages, ablution blocks and a small shop.

The Albasini ruins, 40 kilometres due west of Skukuza, mark the homestead of one of the first white inhabitants of the Lowveld. There is a small display of items discovered when the ruins were excavated some years ago. Shirimantanga hill is a wonderful viewpoint 12 kilometres south of Skukuza, off the Malelane road; there is a plaque commemorating Colonel Stevenson-Hamilton, whose ashes were scattered here. Another lookout is at Granokop, about five kilometres northeast on the Skukuza-Pretoriuskop road.

OPPOSITE, BOTTOM: *Dawn and dusk are heralded by the calling of francolins. Here a Swainson's Francolin proclaims its territory.* ABOVE: *The white rhino was re-established in the Pretoriuskop region in 1961, having disappeared from the Lowveld around 1896. It has subsequently prospered and the Park now hosts a major population of this once-endangered species.*

CHAINS OF LIFE

THE AREA BETWEEN ORPEN GATE AND SKUKUZA

Catenas are seldom displayed as clearly as in southern and East Africa. They are best developed on gently rolling topography, in semi-arid climates, on geologies like the Lowveld that generate a mixture of coarse and fine particles.

In the 1930s a young English soil scientist, Geoffrey Milne, was asked to map the soils of East Africa, a vast area, much of which was inaccessible wilderness. After a few years he noted that the same combinations of soil and vegetation repeated themselves, time after time, over vast areas and in a predictable sequence down a hillslope. Since the vegetation patterns were visible on aerial photographs, the underlying soils could be mapped with a minimum of fieldwork. He called this predictable sequence a catena, from the Latin word for chain. His observation is now universally applied in soil science. When a hole is dug in the ground several different layers, called horizons, are encountered. Typically, the surface is sandier and easier to dig than the underlying soil. This is because the clays have washed out of the topsoil and have been deposited in the subsoil. Moisture in the soil seeps downhill under the influence of gravity, taking with it soluble constituents (including many plant nutrients) and fine, suspended particles.

ABOVE: *Sunset.* LEFT: *The density of giraffe in the central region is among the world's highest.* OPPOSITE: *There are thought to be about 2 000 lions in the Kruger National Park.*

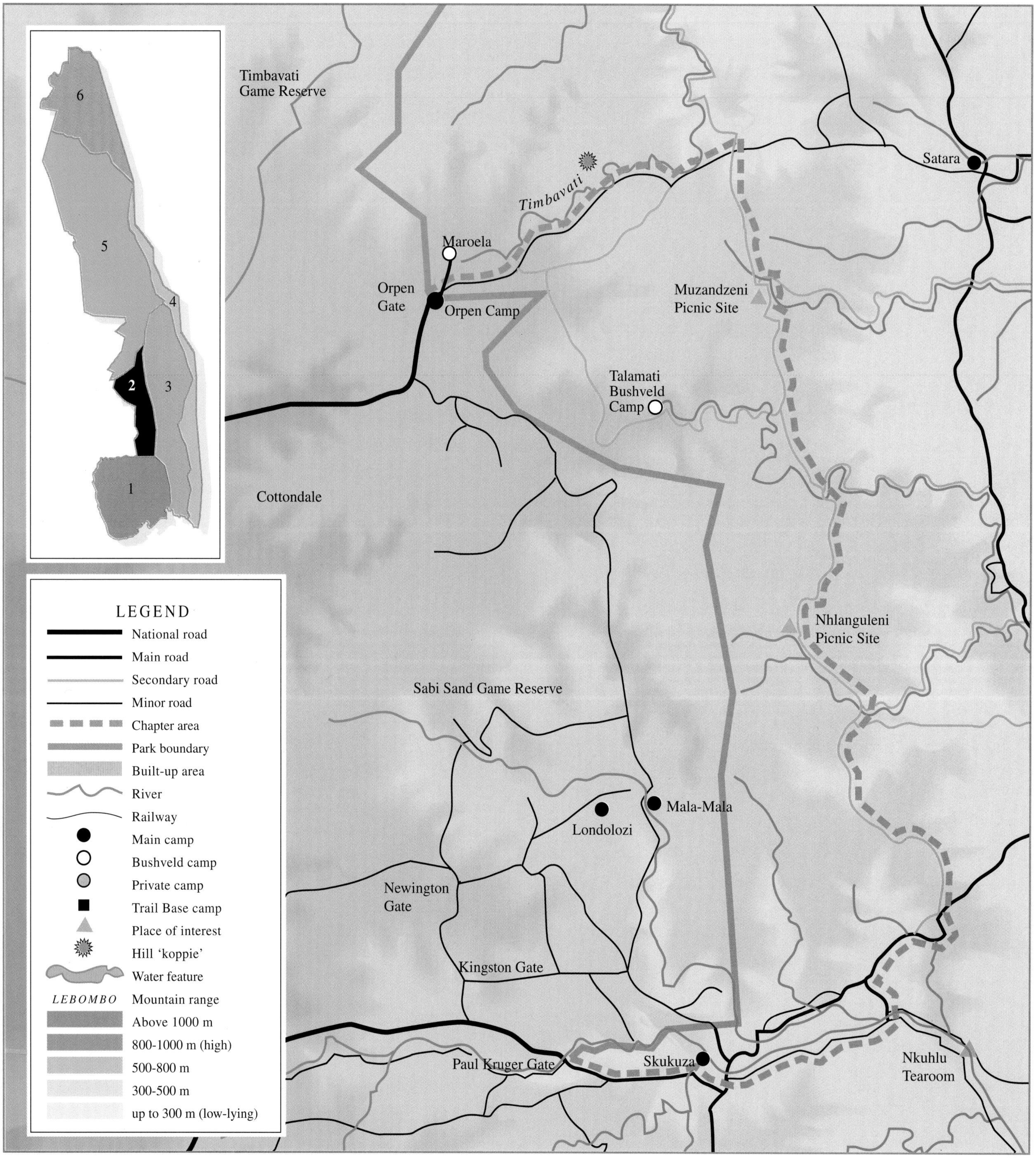
Timbavati
Game Reserve
Timbavati
Maroela
Orpen
Gate
Orpen Camp
Muzandzeni
Picnic Site
Talamati
Bushveld
Camp
Satara
Cottondale
Nhlanguleni
Picnic Site
Sabi Sand Game Reserve
Mala-Mala
Londolozi
Newington
Gate
Kingston Gate
Paul Kruger Gate
Skukuza
Nkuhlu
Tearoom
6
5
4
3
2
1
LEGEND
National road
Main road
Secondary road
Minor road
Chapter area
Park boundary
Built-up area
River
Railway
Main camp
Bushveld camp
Private camp
Trail Base camp
Place of interest
Hill 'koppie'
Water feature
LEBOMBO Mountain range
Above 1000 m
800-1000 m (high)
500-800 m
300-500 m
up to 300 m (low-lying)

In extremely dry climates there is not enough downhill water flow to move the clays and no catenal development occurs. In very wet climates, on the other hand, these materials wash right out of the bottom of the landscape and are lost down the rivers, leaving behind the deep, red, acid, infertile soils that characterize the moist tropics. In semi-arid climates, especially if the rainfall is concentrated into one season, the clays and solutes are deposited in the valley bottoms, resulting in distinctive catenas[15].

Sodic Sites

Sodic sites often look terribly bare and eroded. However, they are a natural part of the Lowveld landscape and have certain advantages provided that they do not expand excessively. For instance, sodic soils, due to their watertightness, are where the temporary wallows and waterholes form. Animals congregate on them, partly because the absence of grass makes predators easy to detect and partly in search of salt. While plants do not need sodium, animals do. In fact, animals seldom get enough sodium from the plants they eat and almost always crave salt. The plants on sodic sites contain more sodium than vegetation elsewhere and besides relishing sodic-site plants, animals are known to lick the soil too[6].

BELOW: *Cheetahs are sometimes referred to as 'the greyhounds of cats' – they are the fastest animals on earth over a short distance. Cheetahs are tall and slender with long legs and a short muzzle on a distinctly rounded head. Generally, these cats stand about 80 centimetres at the shoulders, though their erectile crest of hair may give a taller impression. The coats of cheetahs are elegantly spotted.*

Clay is the storehouse of plant nutrients. It allows humus, the main source of nitrogen, phosphorus and sulphur for plants, to accumulate in the soil. Clay controls the physical properties of soil, such as how much water it retains. Too much clay results in problems like waterlogging in the wet season and extreme aridity in the dry season.

Clay particles are crystals that form in the soil by the recombination of dissolved elements. The crystal lattices are only a few atoms thick

LEFT: *It has been discovered in several parts of Africa that hyaenas are not the cowardly scavengers they were once thought to be. Instead, it appears that these animals are among the main predators in the wild, and that lions in fact do much of the scavenging.* OPPOSITE, BELOW: *Kori Bustards are the largest bustards in southern Africa. During the breeding season, visitors to the Park might spot a male ballooning out its breast feathers in display.*

LEFT: *Because the height at which giraffe feed is around five metres, they have few direct competitors in the wild for their food resources. There are also not many predators that can successfully tackle such a large animal. Despite this, their numbers have never necessitated the culling of giraffe in the Kruger National Park.*

but thousands of atoms wide. This gives clay lattices a huge surface area for their mass. The crystal lattice has a slightly imbalanced electrical charge and the surface of the clay bears a small negative charge. Many plant nutrients are positively charged cations. Since opposite charges attract, these nutrients are held on the clay surface until they are needed by the plants.

TABLE 2

The number and biomass ('living mass') of herbivores in the Kruger Park. The numbers have been averaged for the decade 1982-1992, but not corrected for undercounting. This is therefore a conservative estimate: in the case of animals such as impala, the true number is probably twice what is reflected here, and for warthog it may be ten times higher. The mean mass is taken to be the mean adult female mass. LSU stands for 'Large Stock Unit', the equivalent of a healthy 450 kg steer. (Source: Annual Report of National Parks Board.)

SPECIES	NUMBERS OF ANIMALS	MEAN MASS (kg)	LSU/ ANIMAL	LSU EQUIVALENTS
ELEPHANT	7 579	3 300	5.00	37 895
HIPPO	2 596	1 320	2.00	5 192
BUFFALO	29 242	530	1.32	38 599
ROAN	300	240	0.53	159
SABLE	2 022	200	0.50	1 011
ELAND	635	500	1.16	737
TSESSEBE	926	113	0.36	336
GIRAFFE	5 051	850	1.73	8 753
WATERBUCK	3 436	160	0.49	1 677
WILDEBEEST	13 285	115	0.51	6 789
ZEBRA	29 995	290	0.79	23 546
IMPALA	125 444	45	0.19	23 207
KUDU	8 735	160	0.52	4 507
NYALA	296	62	0.20	59
WHITE RHINO	1 000	1 600	3.50	3 500
BLACK RHINO	50	880	1.60	80
WARTHOG	2 580	65	0.27	691
TOTAL				156 738

TOP: *Lappetfaced Vulture at a kill.* ABOVE AND RIGHT: *Lions at work and at play.* OPPOSITE, TOP: *The sharp claws of oxpeckers are tolerated in exchange for the service they provide in picking off parasites.* OPPOSITE, BELOW: *Vigilance is essential for the survival of baboons.*

When clay crystals form in soils that are rich in aluminium but poor in silicon, the lattice is built with one silicon atom per aluminium atom. This results in a class of clays with a relatively low surface area and surface charge. Soils dominated by these clays are less fertile. Clays which form in the silicon-rich valleys have two silicon atoms per aluminium atom, forming a three-layer sandwich. These clays, called smectites, have a huge surface area and charge, and are very fertile. They also swell when wet. In the Kruger Park catenas, the ridge-top soils contain a small amount of the first type of clay and the valley soils contain a large amount of the second type. This accounts for most of their dramatic differences in vegetation.

Another factor that helps to make the catenas in the Kruger Park so distinctive is the influence of sodium. The granites of the Lowveld contain sodium-rich feldspar, which releases sodium as the rock weathers. It is not generally needed by plants, so it is not retained by the vegetation. On its way down the slope the sodium does some very peculiar things to the clays.

Sodium bears a positive charge like the other cations but it is a larger atom. When it muscles into the space between the clay particles, it prevents them from forming the clumps that let water seep through. Very small changes in the concentration of sodium can therefore alter the soil from porous and penetrable, to watertight and impenetrable. Soils affected

in this way are said to be 'sodic'. They occur towards the valley bottoms, are usually light-coloured, have a surface as hard as concrete and are often bare of grasses. Sodic sites have expanded dramatically in the last few decades. This expansion can usually be linked to poorly sited roads or water points.

The sodium-dispersed clay soil acts as a dam within the soil. Water moving downslope within the soil is forced to the surface when it reaches the dam, forming the distinctive 'seepline grasslands' which are marshy for a few weeks or months in most years. The grassland itself is usually a strip, ten to fifty metres wide, following the contour of the slope.

When the clay dam is damaged, for example, by cutting through it with a road, the water leaks out of the dam and the seeplines become dry. The dispersed clay is quickly eroded by moving water because the unclumped particles can easily be moved. This erosion takes place below the surface of the soil, and the first visible sign is when the soil above the erosion collapses, forming a gully (or donga).

Sodic soils are apparently ideal places to build dams and water holes. However, large dams and pumped water holes are permanently supplied

ABOVE: *Large numbers of tortoises can often be seen immediately after the spring rains, roaming around slowly and purposefully in search of succulent food and mates. These reptiles lay their eggs underground where they are protected from the fires that rage in the dry season. There are three species of tortoise in the Kruger National Park. Pictured here is a leopard tortoise.* RIGHT: *Spiders are one of the less visible predators of the Kruger National Park. Pictured here are the nest and web of a species of community spider. All occupants of a nest share ensnared prey.*

with water which causes the local herbivore population to rise, exerting pressure on the surrounding vegetation. When stripped of its vegetation cover, topsoil washes away. Therefore, well-intentioned actions have accelerated the rate of soil loss to unnatural levels[6].

Since 1903 game numbers have been steadily rising. Logically, the growth in animal numbers cannot continue indefinitely: sooner or later the grazers would be eating all the available grass. The death rate would rise and the birth rate would fall until they were exactly equal. This theoretical natural upper limit of the herbivore population is called the ecological carrying capacity. If we knew what the long-term ecological carrying capacity was, it would help not only with the management of the Park but also with the sustainable management of cattle grazing systems outside the Park.

Since the late 1970s, the Park's biologists have conducted an annual aerial census of the larger herbivores in the Park. The census of hippos requires flying along all the major rivers in a helicopter. Helicopters are also used to census animals in large herds, such as elephant and buffalo. Other species are counted in narrow strips from low-flying aircraft. This method is accurate to within about five per cent for large, highly visible animals but sees fewer of the smaller species and a tiny fraction of species such as nyala, warthog and steenbok. As a result, the actual numbers of these animals are probably much higher than the official figures which are therefore used to interpret trends rather than total numbers.

Giraffe are large, easily counted, have few direct competitors and their numbers have never been controlled by culling; as such, their population provides a good example for the theory of carrying capacity. Initially, when the animal numbers are low, the population grows exponentially. When the numbers become so high that the giraffe begin to compete with one another for the available food, the growth rate begins to slow down and eventually levels off.

For the whole Kruger Park the ecological carrying capacity for giraffe is about 5 000 animals. The population is self-regulating around this level. Most of them are concentrated in the area between the Sabie and Olifants rivers, which has one of the highest densities of these animals in the world.

Mutual Grooming

Troops of vervet monkeys can number up to 20 or more. It has been found that the desire to groom and to be groomed is an important factor in troop cohesion. Mutual grooming usually occurs after the first feeding session and is usually initiated by the females. It is also practised more often by females than by males; some males never participate in grooming. Mutual grooming is also an important form of social behaviour among baboons and is undertaken to varying degrees by all members of the troop except infants.

The giraffe population is limited by the amount of available browse, especially during the dry season. However, giraffe do not die directly of starvation. Every few years there is an exceptionally cold spell in September, when the giraffe are coincidentally most stressed due to lack of food. Animals in poor condition are very susceptible to diseases; in the case of giraffe large numbers die of pneumonia brought on by the cold and damp. This periodic stress-related mortality keeps the population regulated at a level where there is just enough food for them, without the need for any intervention by Park managers.

The Kruger Park contains many species of browsers. An interesting observation is that there is a rather orderly pattern in the body mass of coexisting browsers. An impala is more or less twice as heavy as a duiker, a nyala twice as heavy as an impala, and so on up through kudu, eland and giraffe. The differences in mass correspond with differences in feeding height. Duiker feed between the ground and about one metre, impala up to 1,8 metres, kudu to 2,5 metres and giraffe to five metres. While there is considerable overlap in these ranges, there is also enough separation to allow a diverse browser community to coexist. Adding new browser species to the ecosystem, therefore, slightly reduces the carrying capacity for other browsers but increases the overall browser carrying capacity as it increases the completeness with which the browse resource is used – one of the ecological arguments for why multi-species herbivore systems should be more productive than, say, cattle-only systems.

Building an ecosystem consisting of plants and herbivores becomes a bit more complicated when grass-eaters (grazers) are also considered. There are many different grazer species competing for food that is within the reach of all the species. There is a degree of niche separation between grazers on the basis of what types of grass they prefer. Together the different species can make better use of the grassland than they would do alone.

The grass plant can be eaten right down to the ground (and below it when the grazer is a grubbing species such as a warthog). Grasses are therefore much more susceptible to overuse than trees are. This makes the subset of the ecosystem consisting of grazers and grasses

HAAK-EN-STEEK

The umbrella thorn (Acacia tortilis) *is one of the most widespread acacias in Africa. This tree may be found growing in dry areas, in relatively fertile soils.*

The Afrikaans common name, haak-en-steek, *which means 'grab and prick', refers to the distinctive thorn pattern of the paired white thorns, which are alternately long and straight and short and hooked.*

The haak-en-steek has a spiral pod which measures about two centimetres in diameter, and which is eagerly eaten by many herbivores, due to its high protein content. Elephants will shake umbrella thorn trees in order to dislodge the pods growing on them, and then they will snack on the fallen pods as if they were popcorn. The seeds, which are protected by tough coats, survive the passage through the digestive system of these huge mammals, and readily germinate after being distributed in the elephants' dung.

OPPOSITE: Contrary to the popular perception that vultures get most of their food by hanging around predator kills, this source accounts for less than one tenth of their food intake.
RIGHT: Wild dogs are illustrated here engaging in rarely photographed 'denning' activities around their den site in a termite mound (centre). The top photograph shows an adult 'ecouraging' a pup to leave the den by dragging it out by its ear.

much less stable than that consisting of browsers and trees. Overgrazing is a widespread problem, both in nature reserves and in the areas outside of them.

The broad categories 'grazer' and 'browser' are an over-simplification, however. All herbivores have a mixed diet to some degree. Animals such as giraffe eat so little grass that one can safely consider them to be pure browsers, but kudu eat a significant quantity of forbs (the non-grass plants which grow among the grasses). Forbs are typically more nutritious than grasses but are often toxic. They are a less reliable food source than perennial grasses but they do help kudu survive during critical times.

There are several species that combine browse and grass in their diet to such a degree that they must be considered 'mixed feeders'. The ability of elephant and impala to switch between food sources is one of the reasons why they are gradually coming to dominate in many conservation areas. In both cases, grass makes up about three-quarters of their diet when it is freely available. During times when there is little grass, tree leaf becomes dominant. At some times of the year flowers and fruit make up a significant part of the diet.

Herbivore numbers are limited not by the total amount of plant material produced by the ecosystem but by the quantity of nutritious, palatable and accessible food. A broad generalization is that grazer numbers are limited by the quality of the grass (in particular, its nitrogen content), while browser numbers are limited by the quantity of available and edible material during the critical period of the late dry season, when most of the trees have lost their leaves.

In order to calculate the carrying capacity for mixtures of different herbivore species it is necessary to reduce all of the species to a common

denominator. A small-bodied herbivore obviously needs less food than a large-bodied animal but relative to its body mass it actually requires much more. The physiological reasons for this have to do with the necessity for mammals to regulate their body temperature within narrow limits. Small-bodied animals have a large surface

ABOVE AND OPPOSITE: *Elephants are mixed feeders, combining browse (leaves and twigs) and grass in their diet.*
LEFT: *The impala lily* (Adenium obesum) *bears magnificent flowers. These are a familiar sight to those who visit the Kruger Park during winter and early spring. The flowers are produced in clusters and appear at the tips of fleshy, swollen, succulent stems.*

area relative to their mass – they therefore require more energy than a larger animal in order to maintain their body temperature.

For convenience, the populations of all the different herbivores are expressed in terms of their appetites. The unit of comparison is the Large Stock Unit (LSU), nominally equivalent to one head of cattle. The total mass of herbivores in the Kruger Park is about 2 140 kilograms per square kilometre, which translates

FENCELINES

During the early 1960s a fence was erected on the western boundary of the Kruger Park to help control the spread of animal diseases. Wild ungulates, especially buffalo and wildebeest, harbour many diseases that can be transmitted to domestic cattle. The reverse is also true: wildlife is susceptible to many cattle diseases. However, migration is one of the main ways in which grazers adapt to seasonal variations in their food supply: they move to an area which has more grass. The ability of the game to migrate from areas of low food supply to those that offer better resources, has been partly restored by the decision to drop the fences between the Park and adjacent wildlife areas. This increases the necessity of managing the entire Lowveld as one unit.

One Large Stock Unit needs ten kilograms of food a day; therefore, all the grazing herbivores in the Park consume about 700 000 tons of grass a year. Since the total amount of grass growing in the Kruger Park in an average year is about two million tons, less than half of the grass is eaten by grazers. This fraction varies from place to place.

Clearly, the grazers are not limited by the absolute amount of food but by the grass that they are able to reach and digest. It would not be desirable for the grazers to eat all the grass on offer, since some is needed to support other herbivores (such as insects, which in some situations eat more grass than the large mammals) and to protect the soil against erosion.

In historical times the grass available to water-dependent species was limited to that which was within about five kilometres of drinking water. The herbivore populations were kept at a level well below that needed for complete consumption of the grass by the sparse and shifting distribution of water. For this reason many of the major species were migratory, giving the grass a chance to recover between episodes of intense grazing, a pattern of consumption to which African grasses are well adapted. Unlike trees, grasses have no trunk in which to store water; grass growth is therefore completely dependent on rainfall. If the rains

into approximately 200 000 'cattle equivalents' for the whole Park, or one LSU per ten hectares. This is slightly higher than the stocking density that would be recommended for a cattle ranch in the Lowveld, but is substantially fewer animals than the maximum number that could be kept on such an area of land (at least in the short term) based on calculations of the amount of available plant material.

One of the reasons that the Kruger National Park is still not 'full' is because there remain areas which are not completely utilized due to the absence of drinking water during the dry season. This protects the Park from the wild swings in animal numbers that occur where the animal densities are high everywhere in the landscape. Another reason that the Park is below its maximum ecological carrying capacity is that predators such as lion, hyaena, leopard and cheetah keep the herbivore populations slightly below their maximum.

OPPOSITE: *White Helmetshrikes are usually seen in small groups, foraging for insects in* Acacia *savannas.*
LEFT: Xerophyta retinervis *is appropriately named 'baboon's tail'. It is an indicator of shallow soils. In spring the blackened stumps come to life and delicate flowers appear at their tips. They survive frequent burning.*
ABOVE: *The white syringa* (Kirkia acuminata) *in the foreground is not related to red syringas* (Burkea africana) *and, ironically, neither are syringa trees. These two species are representatives of the main core of broad-leaved savannas on the infertile soils of south-central Africa which are known as miombo woodlands.*

are good, the grass production is high; if they are bad, the grass crop is poor. Browse production by trees also fluctuates between years but to a much lesser degree since there is some carry-over of water and energy from previous years. Two human actions have altered significantly the ecology of herbivores in the Lowveld in the last half century. The first was the provision of many permanent water points where none had previously existed; the second was the erection of fences, primarily for veterinary purposes, which stopped animal movement. The first action greatly increased the short-term carrying capacity of the Lowveld by removing water limitations in vast areas and allowing the animal numbers to rise to a ceiling imposed by food limitations. The grass food supply in the Lowveld fluctuates by about 30 per cent per year. The ability of the animal populations to absorb that variation without massive die-offs has been greatly reduced by the fences which prevent them from migrating into areas which have received better rainfall. The provision of water means that the animal populations are high everywhere, and there is nowhere for them to migrate to. The consequences become apparent during the droughts that occur every decade or so in the Lowveld, during which large numbers of herbivores die.

Times of famine for herbivores are times of feast for scavengers. One of the important ecological features of the Kruger Park is that it still has an almost intact community of scavengers; in many other parts of South Africa this community is absent or reduced due to habitat loss and the poisoning of carcasses.

SAUSAGE TREE

*The sausage tree (*Kigelia africana*) is very appropriately named as its fruits hanging from the branches closely resemble sausages. They contain mostly fibre but are eaten by elephants and other animals. However, the fruits are poisonous to man – especially when unripe – although the roasted seeds are eaten by some indigenous tribes.*

The attractive burgundy flowers are borne on robust stalks and hang free of the foliage. This facilitates their pollination by bats. The fruits develop slowly after the blooms have been pollinated. Sausage trees are generally found near to rivers or drainage lines.

Researchers in the Kruger National Park have documented 224 species of insect which are attracted to carcasses, including 100 species of beetle and 87 species of fly. The most important are the blowflies. The green variety arrive first at a kill and their maggots dominate the carcass initially. In time, however, the blue variety breeds faster and ends up consuming the others. Left to their own devices these maggots will reduce an impala-sized carcass to clean bones in five days; at their peak, the carcass will contain over 200 000 maggots! Fortunately, this is seldom the case, since vultures usually find the carcass and consume it before the fly eggs can hatch. In this way vultures perform an important sanitation task.

By the evening of the first day, the carcass will begin to smell, attracting jackals, hyaenas and a host of other carrion-eaters. Among the animals seen feeding on carcasses are mongooses, leguaans and warthogs. If for some reason these scavengers fail to find it, the carcass will become a slimy, heaving mass of maggots by the end of the second day, at which stage it is no

BELOW: *Although kudu are browsers that feed at a height of two-and-a-half metres, they also eat the broad-leaved plants growing within the grass layer, especially in the springtime. Kudu are accomplished jumpers and can leap a two-metre fence with ease – Stevenson-Hamilton had to raise his garden wall to three metres to keep them out. These antelope are wasteful raiders of certain crops. They are fond of mealies and tobacco and can do a great deal of damage in vegetable farms and gardens.*

longer attractive to vultures, although many species of the smaller birds will feast on the maggots. Vultures, therefore, must find the carcass and consume it on the first day after death. The task of locating a single carcass in thousands of hectares of savanna might seem impossible. Vultures apparently achieve this not by looking for carcasses, but by watching other vultures. The carcass is usually first found by a Bateleur or Whiteheaded Vulture, both of which cruise 50 to 100 metres above the ground. Their change in behaviour is detected by Lappetfaced and Hooded Vultures circling at approximately 200 metres in altitude. These birds are in turn monitored by the high-flying Cape and Whitebacked Vultures. This pyramid allows hundreds of vultures to converge on the carcass from 20 or more kilometres away, within minutes of the first bird arriving. Those birds that come from high up and far away must be able to fly very fast. This speed factor has been demonstrated by the timing of Cape Vultures, which have been clocked diving at 140 kilometres an hour for their food.

The first arrivals do not simply fly directly to the carcass and begin feeding; they perch in the vicinity for a while and watch for danger. Eventually one, usually a Whiteheaded Vulture or a Bateleur, will fly down and peck at the carcass. Others soon follow. They have only a few

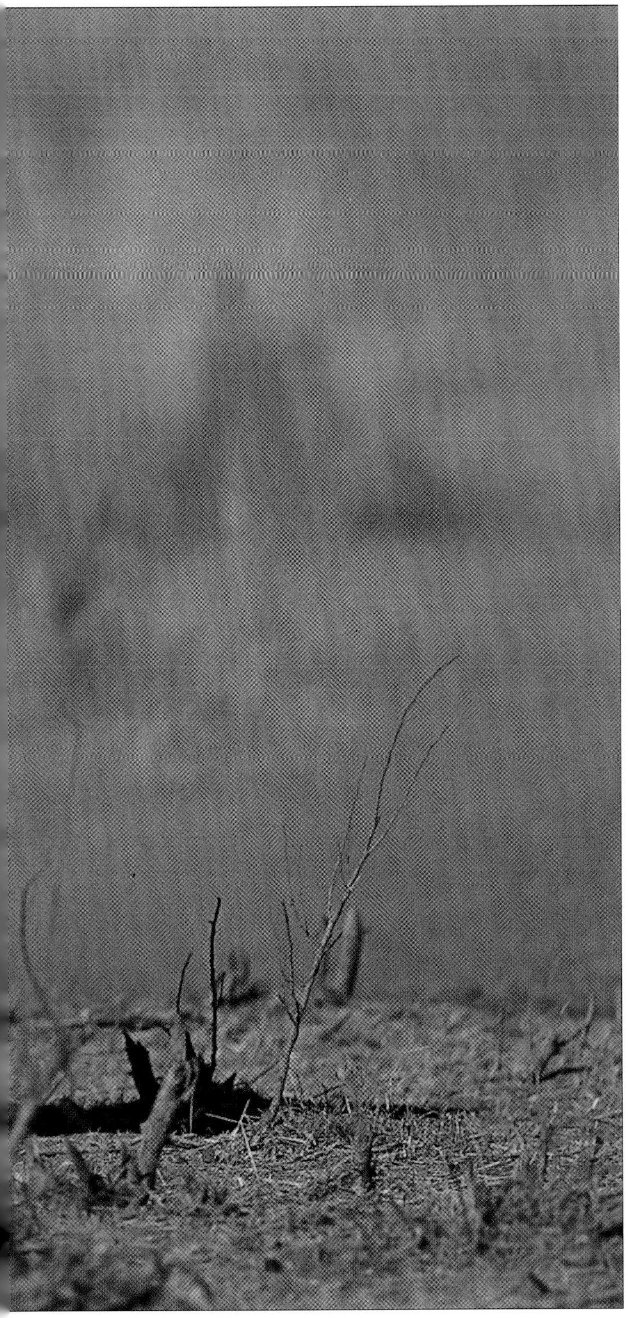

minutes to feed before the numerous waiting griffons (Cape and Whitebacked Vultures) pile in simultaneously as if reacting to a signal. It is the griffons, with their powerful necks and hooked beaks, that do most of the dirty work of opening up the carcass. The competition for food within the jostling mass of griffons is fierce, and the Bateleurs and Whitefaced Vultures are pushed aside. The griffons are each able to consume one to one-and-a-half kilograms of meat within five minutes, before they are in turn displaced by the larger (but less numerous) Lappetfaced Vultures. The griffons then retire to preen – their cropful of meat will last them three days or more. It is the multitude of fast-flying griffons that get the bulk of the prize; the Lappetfaced Vultures are specialized to feed on the outside of the carcass and they tear the sinews off the bone at their leisure.

Tourist Facilities in the Western-Central Kruger Park

Accommodation

Excluding Skukuza, which is on the border of this region and a good base from which to explore it, there is only one small restcamp, two bushveld camps and one campsite. Orpen Camp is small and pleasant (44 beds). It is located at Orpen Gate. Maroela Campsite is close by and was specially designed for caravans and tents; it can accommodate up to 120 people. The Talamati Bushveld Camp is small, rustic, and has a minimum of facilities – a good place for peace and quiet. It has ten six-bedded and five four-bedded cottages. The bushveld camp at Jakkalsbessie is the only small camp with conference facilities. It sleeps a maximum of 32, in huts and cottages.

Places of Interest

On the Orpen-to-Satara road there are two pull-offs where visitors can look down on the Timbavati River – a good perspective from which to watch elephants or buffalo. Visitors may get out of their vehicles at the lookout closer to Satara. They may also do so at Timbavati, a picnic site 32 kilometres further north on the Timbavati River. There is another picnic site at Nhlanguleni, situated approximately half way between Skukuza and Orpen Gate, on road S36. A third picnic spot is located at Muzandzeni, halfway between Nhlanguleni and Orpen Gate.

Opposite and Right: *All the zebra in the Park are Burchell's zebra, distinguished by the faint brownish shadow-stripes between the main black bands. One theory to explain the startling coat of the zebra, which hardly qualifies as camouflage, is that in a herd the shifting patterns produce a dazzling optical illusion which makes it difficult for predators to single out an individual for attack.*
Opposite, Below: *The Black Flycatcher might easily be mistaken for a Forktailed Drongo. The latter is slightly larger and has a red eye.*

THE FERTILE PLAINS

THE LANDSCAPE BETWEEN CROCODILE BRIDGE AND OLIFANTS CAMP

For sheer numbers of animals, the richest part of the Kruger National Park is the belt of flat country immediately west of the Lebombos, between Crocodile Bridge in the south and Olifants Camp in the north.

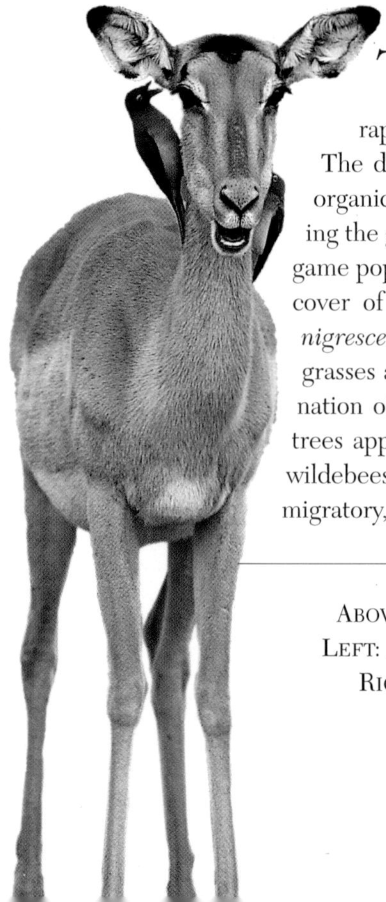

The reason for the flatness of this landscape is that this strip of land is underlain by basalts. Basalt weathers relatively rapidly, leaving no hills, but generating a clayey, nutrient-rich soil. The dark colour of the soil is due to the relatively high amount of organic matter it contains. This provides nitrogen to the plants, causing the grasses to be nutritious throughout the year, and leads to a high game population. At first glance the plains appear to have a fairly sparse cover of trees. The dominant tree species are knob thorns (*Acacia nigrescens*) and marula trees (*Sclerocarya birrea*). Hidden among the grasses are many small trees, prevented from growing tall by a combination of browsing and fire. Where fire is excluded a dense stand of trees appears. The basalt plains are home to large herds of zebra and wildebeest, often seen grazing together. The wildebeest herds were once migratory, like those found in the Kalahari Desert and on the plains of the

ABOVE: *A young male waterbuck wading into a water hole to drink.*
LEFT: *Female impala with oxpecker gleening parasites from her hide.*
RIGHT: *Zebra are typical animals of the open plains of the Kruger National Park. They concentrate in this region in winter.*

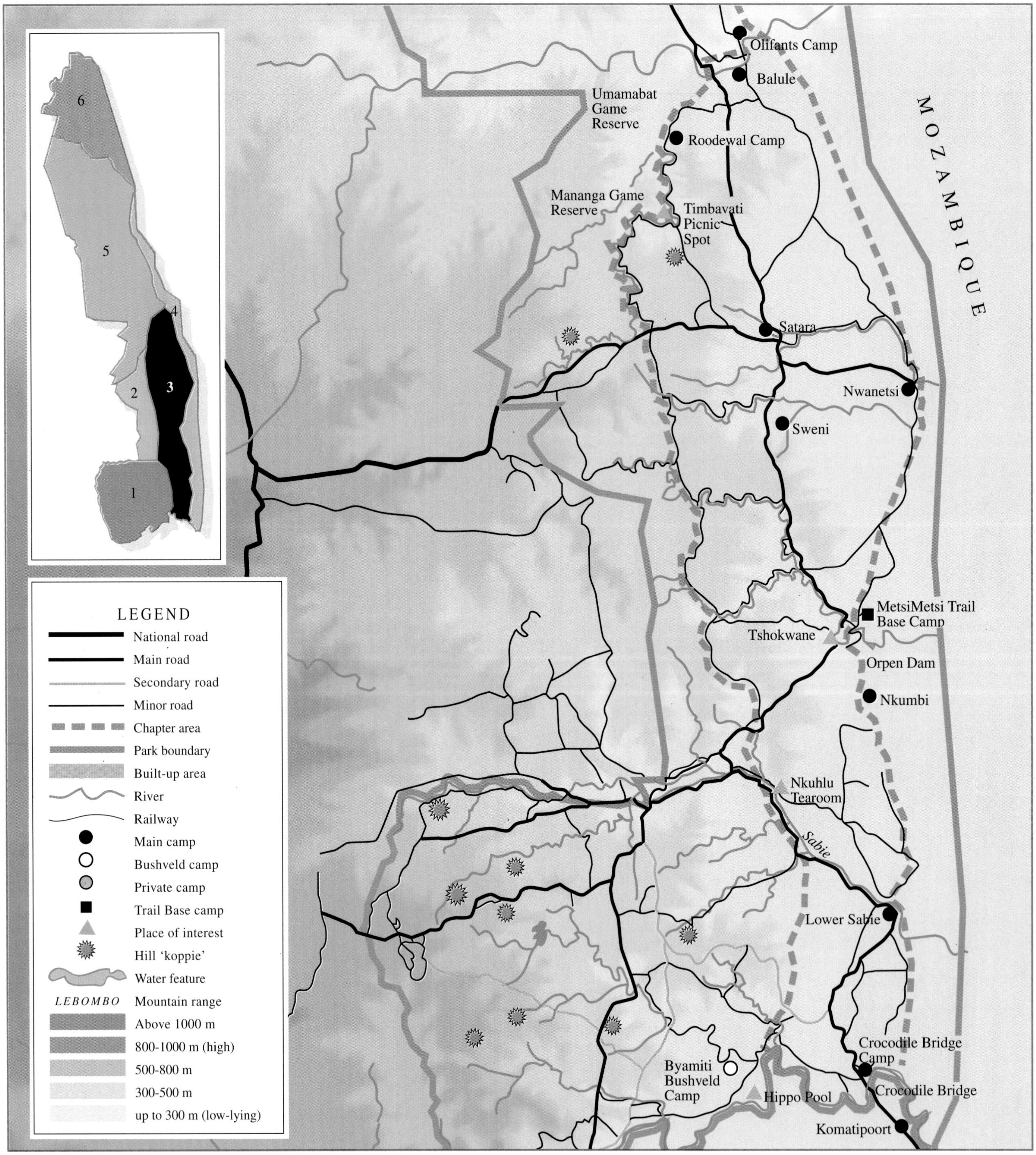
6
5
4
3
2
1
LEGEND
National road
Main road
Secondary road
Minor road
Chapter area
Park boundary
Built-up area
River
Railway
Main camp
Bushveld camp
Private camp
Trail Base camp
Place of interest
Hill 'koppie'
Water feature
LEBOMBO Mountain range
Above 1000 m
800-1000 m (high)
500-800 m
300-500 m
up to 300 m (low-lying)
Olifants Camp
Balule
Umamabat Game Reserve
Roodewal Camp
Mananga Game Reserve
Timbavati Picnic Spot
MOZAMBIQUE
Satara
Nwanetsi
Sweni
MetsiMetsi Trail Base Camp
Tshokwane
Orpen Dam
Nkumbi
Nkuhlu Tearoom
Sabie
Lower Sabie
Crocodile Bridge Camp
Crocodile Bridge
Byamiti Bushveld Camp
Hippo Pool
Komatipoort

GRASSES

Grass is the fuel that powers the engine of the Lowveld ecosystems. Rangers use the species composition of the grasslands as a guide to their management. Grasslands in peak condition will be dominated by perennial, palatable species such as Themeda triandra *and the shade-loving* Panicum maximum. *Drought and overgrazing lead to dominance by fibrous annual species such as* Aristida congesta. *The infertile soils of high rainfall areas support unpalatable species such as* Hyperthelia dissoluta, *while fertile soils may support* Urochloa mossambicensis.

BELOW: *Research has shown that giraffe are highly preferred prey of lions. This might have something to do with the fact that their carcasses are so large that they are easily spotted and therefore seldom overlooked when data on kills are being collected.*

Serengeti, but on a smaller scale. During the spring they would leave the plains for the wetter areas to the west, along the foothills of the escarpment. In the early dry season they would return to their winter grazing on the plains.

During the early 1960s a fence was erected on the western boundary of the Kruger Park to prevent this migration. The motivation was to help control the spread of animal diseases. Of particular concern to the cattle industry is foot-and-mouth disease, which is not usually lethal in cattle but prevents the export of meat products. The fence on the western boundary was intended to separate the herds of the eastern Lowveld, where foot-and-mouth disease is always present to a small degree in the game populations, from those of the western Lowveld, where it undergoes only sporadic outbreaks. A second fence further to the west separates the game in the 'outbreak' areas from cattle on commercial ranches, which are supposedly foot-and-mouth free. No meat or untreated animal products may be transported across these lines.

During the 1960s the wildebeest population was stable at approximately 15 000 animals, despite the fence and the severe drought. Concerned by the impact that the wildebeest herd was having on the grasslands in the Kruger Park, the Park authorities culled several thousand in 1969 and 1970. Between 1971 and 1976, which marked a period of good rains, wildebeest numbers plummeted to 7 000. The zebra herd also decreased dramatically. Was the fence across the

RIGHT: *Tourists visiting the Kruger National Park are almost certain to see lions. They may even be lucky enough to witness a kill. Interestingly, a large part of the water requirements of lions can be met by the rumen fluid of their prey. Lions can go without drinking for up to nine days.* OPPOSITE: *A lioness moves in for the kill.*

migration route the cause of the decline or was the reduction in numbers simply related to the change in climate?

Research soon showed that when the wildebeest were culled, the lion numbers were not similarly reduced, so the balance of predators to prey was altered. The wildebeest were further disadvantaged by the unusually tall grass that grew following the good rains. Antelope divide into two groups on the basis of the strategy they have for improving the survival of their offspring soon after birth. The 'leavers', including impala, kudu and giraffe, hide the newborn calves in thick bush or long grass for a few days, until they are strong enough to keep up with the herd. The 'followers', including wildebeest and tsessebe, produce calves that can run as fast as the adults within minutes of being born. Wildebeest survival is favoured by short-grass conditions that allow them to see predators at a distance and run away.

Beginning in 1974 predators were culled (for the first and last time since the early 1950s) in the central part of the Kruger Park. Between 1974 and 1980 over 400 lions and 350 hyaenas were shot – less than a fifth of the lions and hyaenas in the Park and probably no more than a third of the large predators in the central region. The wildebeest and zebra populations began to recover, and have now reached their former levels. The recovery may have had more to do with the change of climate back to a drier phase during the late 1970s and the adjustment of lion numbers and feeding behaviour to the lower number of wildebeest, than to the relatively small number of predators removed.

It seems self-evident that the number of predators has a direct impact on the prey population, but the reality is a little more complicated. Predator control has been part of the management of many parks, including Kruger during its early days. Wildlife managers all around the world have gradually learned that

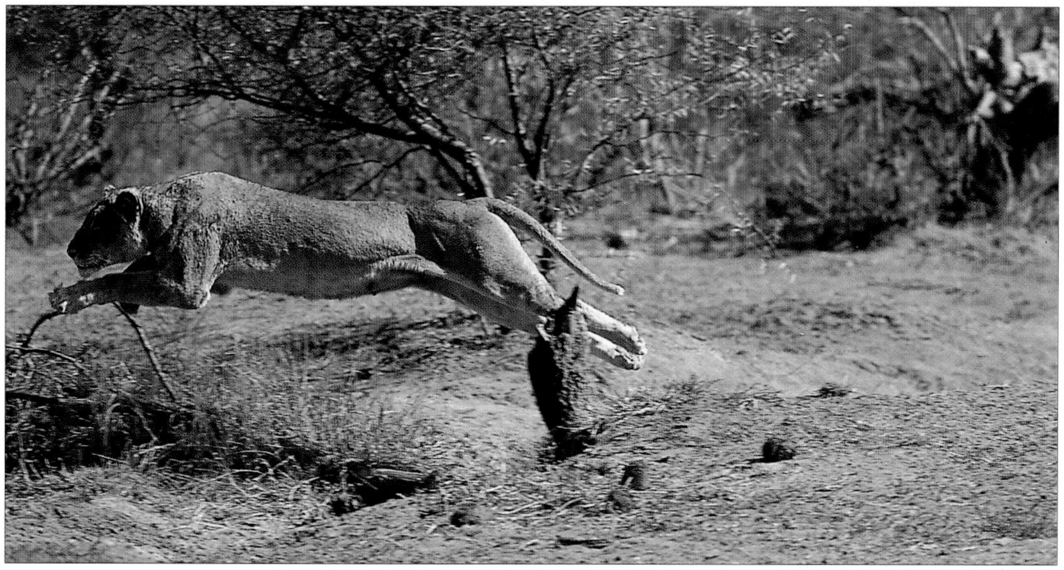

predation is usually not the ultimate factor controlling prey populations and often more problems are caused by well-meaning intervention than by leaving things to sort themselves out.

The example of the lions and wildebeest shows how difficult it is to predict the consequences of interfering with even a relatively simple ecological system, such as lion-eats-wildebeest. It also shows that several factors interact to determine the prey numbers: in this case, the climate, the area of the home range and the preferences of predators for particular types of prey.

Predators do not generally cause the extinction of their prey – that would be evolutionary suicide. However, the predator-prey relationship is a fairly unstable one, characterized by large oscillations. This is especially true when the predators have a high breeding rate relative to the prey. Wildebeest females generally produce only one calf each per year, whereas a lioness can have up to six cubs in a litter. Most of these cubs die of starvation or are killed by other lions. When food is abundant, for instance when wildebeest numbers are high, the result is the survival of more lion cubs. It is only two years later, when these cubs begin to hunt effectively for themselves, that the increase in predators begins to have a feedback effect on the wildebeest population.

In the meantime, the prey numbers begin to stabilize as they approach their carrying capacity. Due to the time-lag and the rapid reproduction rate of lions, the lion population increases beyond the number that can be supported by the prey population, so the latter begins to decline. Again there is a one- or two-year delay before this is registered by the lion population, and this is why predator and prey populations tend to oscillate. Small human interventions, such as culling wildebeest at the same time that the lion population is peaking, can accentuate these fluctuations.

Adding more species of prey to the mix – for instance, giving the lions a choice between eating zebra or wildebeest – usually makes the system less stable rather than more stable due to the fact that lions and other predators develop a preference for particular prey species. While they are capable of switching to alternative species (for instance, lions switch from wildebeest to buffalo when wet climatic phases give

way to drier phases), this behavioural change is gradual and it adds another destabilizing time-lag to the system.

Predator preferences are partly influenced by the ease with which the different species can be captured and the size of meal they provide, but are also partly due to learned behaviour. This does not stop young predators, and lion cubs in particular, from chasing all sorts of unsuitable prey, usually with little success. Individual predators tend to specialize on just a few species, usually the ones that were the main part of their diet when they were learning to hunt.

The prey preferences can be quantified by calculating the ratio of the proportion of kills of a certain species to the proportion of that prey species in the total prey population[17]. For instance, if there are ten wildebeest to every zebra in the area, but zebra make up one lion kill in five, then lions are apparently not hunting at random but focusing a disproportionate amount of effort on zebras. If the ratio is greater than one, it suggests the prey species is preferred; if it is less than one, it is avoided.

There are two sources of data on kills. The Park staff, in the course of its patrols, note all the kills encountered. The rangers try to work

Opposite and Centre Right: *The buffalo population of the Park is kept at about 30 000 by culling.*
Top, Right: *The blue wildebeest is widespread in southern and East Africa. Their large noses make them prone to a disease called 'malignant catarrh' which can be transmitted to cattle.*
Bottom, Right: *Grey Lourie.*

out what species of predator was responsible and the age, sex and species of the prey (by examining the skull). The rangers report this information every month, so the number of records is very high. The problem with these data is that small prey items, such as impala and warthog, are more difficult to find than large carcasses, such as buffalo, so the contribution of smaller animals to the diet is underestimated. A further complication is that this method documents only the successful hunting attempts but misses the failures – which are usually more frequent. According to this method, buffalo, giraffe and kudu are the preferred prey species of lions.

LEFT: *Dawn on the fertile African plains*

A less biased method of collecting prey statistics is to put radio collars on a number of predators and follow them around, day and night, for a long period of time. Every prey item they attempt to kill is noted, along with their success rate. The drawback of this approach is that it is so labour-intensive and expensive that it is possible to collect only a small amount of data, from one area of the Park. Data from this source reveal some surprising information: the preferred prey species of lions are porcupine, warthog and wildebeest. Both types of data agree that giraffe are highly favoured, and impala are avoided by lions. Zebra are neither favoured nor disfavoured, but eaten in the proportion in which they are encountered. Another interesting comparison is between the kill records collected by rangers during the 1960s and in the late 1980s. Lions show similar preferences for kudu and giraffe in both the earlier and later records, while consistently disfavouring impala. However, waterbuck, wildebeest and sable were much more highly preferred in the 1960s, while warthog, eland, tsessebe and roan were preferred in the 1980s.

Predator-prey systems with several alternative prey species are self-stabilizing when the preferred prey species also happens to be both present in the largest numbers and to have the highest reproduction rate. The presence of this readily available and preferred prey species helps to protect the rarer prey species.

Problems arise, however, when the preferred species is the rarer, less fecund species. As a result of an alternative prey species being present to sustain the predators, the feedback loop from the declining prey numbers to the predator population is weakened, and the rarer prey species can therefore be driven to local extinction before the predators are able to 'unlearn' their hunting pattern.

The major predators in the Kruger National Park are lions, hyaenas, leopards, wild dogs and cheetahs. Hyaenas are not purely scavengers, as is widely believed: about half of their diet in Kruger appears to be derived from animals they have killed themselves, making them second only to lions as major predators in the Park – of comparable rank to leopards.

LEADWOOD

The leadwood tree (Combretum imberbe) *has wood with a density of 1 200 kilograms per cubic metre, and will therefore sink if placed in water. The high-density wood is a consequence of the extreme slowness with which the tree grows; a large individual is probably many centuries old. The wood is highly resistant to decay. Dead stumps will stand for decades, providing roosting sites and homes for a wide variety of hole-dwelling creatures. The dead logs are usually finally consumed by fire. They smoulder without a flame for days, leaving only an ashen ghost where once a very sturdy and ancient tree stood.*

Leadwood was once the main fuel supply for all the wood-burning stoves and barbecue facilities in the Park, leading to concern that the dead wood might disappear from the ecosystem. Wood is no longer collected within the Park; the wood on sale in the rest-camps is brought from outside the Park.

The leadwood can easily be identified as a species of Combretum *since it bears the characteristic four-winged seed pods, which in this case are papery, straw-coloured and about one centimetre in length.*

When pods are not present, the finely squared, grey bark is the most distinctive feature. The young branches sprout spine-tipped twigs at right angles to each other and to the main stem, but this characteristic is lost once the trees grow above the reach of browsing animals.

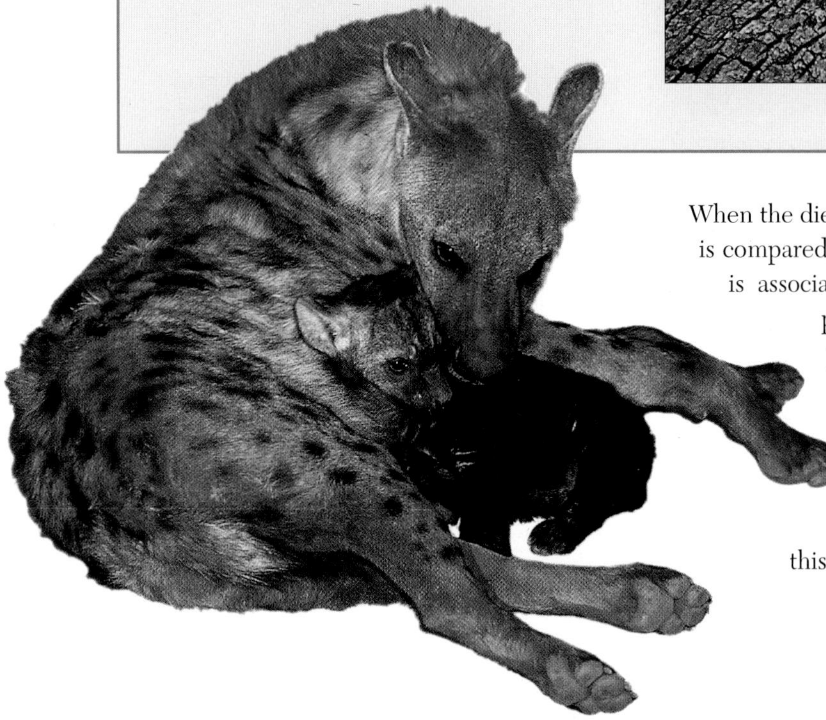

When the diet of each of the major predators is compared, the basic pattern that emerges is associated with the body size of the predator relative to that of the prey. Buffalo, giraffe and sable are essentially attacked only by lions. This does not mean that lions do not also eat smaller prey; bear in mind that the kill records (on which this analysis is based) are biased against small prey items, which are often completely consumed before they are found. A significant fraction of the lion diet is derived from these smaller animals, such as warthog.

Wild dogs, which hunt cooperatively in packs, can kill surprisingly large animals. They occasionally prey on kudu, waterbuck and reedbuck, but most of their diet consists of impala. The wild dog hunting technique is to single out an individual, and then chase it in relays until it is exhausted. The kill is performed by the wild

OPPOSITE: *The social groups of the spotted hyaena are dominated by females. They are larger than their male counterparts, and have a strange 'pseudo-penis', which makes telling them apart from the males difficult, and led to the belief that they are hermaphroditic.*
RIGHT: *During the six or so nights of the full moon in May, the bush resounds with the grunts, snorts and roars of rutting impalas, a most intimidating sound to the uninitiated.*

dogs tearing at the soft underbelly and disembowelling the prey. Wild dogs sometimes kill more prey than they can eat, as do other large predators when faced with abundant prey.

Many predators will start feeding on the entrails before they eat the other parts of their prey. In the case of large, thick-skinned animals such as giraffe and buffalo, the belly is the easiest point of entry into the body. In other cases it is believed that the predators balance their diet in this way. The liver in particular is a rich source of vitamins.

Cheetahs are fast, light-bodied predators, and would risk serious injury if they attacked large prey items; impala are the major component of their diet. Kudu, waterbuck and reedbuck are also taken, but generally immature individuals are selected. Unlike leopards, cheetahs are unable to protect their kill against robbers. They gulp down several kilograms of meat before they are chased off the kill by other predators or scavengers. Although cheetahs can accelerate very rapidly and are the swiftest predators over short distances, they have little stamina. The hunting technique employed by cheetahs is to stalk to within a short distance of their prey and then to rush at it.

Most studies in Africa have estimated that there are between 15 and 35 kills per member of the lion population per year. This does not mean that every lion kills this many times in a year; adult lions are more successful hunters than juveniles, and the females tend to hunt more than the males. The number of kills per lion in the Kruger Park is probably towards the lower side of this estimate, because the prey items are relatively large. The 'average' leopard is thought to kill about 20 times in a year, the 'average' cheetah about 26 times a year, and the 'average' wild dog about 50 times a year.

Assuming that there are approximately 2 000 lions, 1 000 leopards, 400 wild dogs and 200 cheetah in the Kruger Park, this means that about 76 000 large herbivores are killed and eaten in the Kruger Park every year.

This rough calculation implies that, on average, about one herbivore in ten will become food for a lion in a given year. If we add the other large predators (leopard, hyaena, wild dog and cheetah), the fraction of the population that meets a violent end in a given year rises to about one in four. This is close to, but just below, the natural reproduction rate of the herbivores. The size of the herbivore population is determined primarily by their food supply and less so by predation. The size of the predator

OPPOSITE, LEFT: *Tree agama in a weeping boer bean tree (*Scotia brachypetala*).*
OPPOSITE, TOP RIGHT: *Rhino seldom fall prey to predators.*
OPPOSITE, BOTTOM RIGHT: *The Hooded Vulture is associated with humans in North and West Africa, but not in southern Africa. It is adept at sneaking morsels from predators or other vultures.*
ABOVE: *Sable, due to their size and their dangerously sharp horns, are essentially only attacked by lions.*
LEFT: *Mopane pomegranate (*Rhigozum zambesiacum*) burst into beautiful flower after the first rains.*

CHEETAHS

Cheetahs are commonest in the southern part of the Kruger Park, especially in the open savanna between Satara and Crocodile Bridge.

These graceful animals weigh only approximately 50 kilograms (which is a quarter of the mass of a lion), and their build is adapted to short, fast pursuit. The long, thick tail is an essential counterbalance and it allows cheetahs to manoeuvre at great speed.

Impala are their preferred prey species and the major component of their diet. Kudu, waterbuck and reedbuck are also taken, but generally immature individuals are selected.

Their hunting technique is to stalk to within a short distance of their prey and then to rush at it and chase it down.

population rises to the level which can, in turn, be supported by its food supply; in this case the number of herbivores.

The prey population therefore generally determines the size of the predator population, and not vice versa. At equilibrium, the predators are simply living off the excess animals in the prey population; in doing so they depress the prey population below the ecological carrying capacity, probably by about one fifth in the case of the Kruger Park. However, as has been noted, the system is seldom (if ever) at equilibrium. Given that nearly a quarter of the herbivore population can be eaten in a given year, it takes a time-lag of only two years to halve it.

The relationship between predator numbers and prey numbers is seldom direct and simple. Apart from the complications introduced by multiple prey and predators, time-lags, as well as learned behaviours, most predators have mechanisms that help to regulate their numbers. Such mechanisms are known as density-dependent population regulators and they work by establishing a feedback directly from the predator population density to its population growth rate, thereby reducing the time-lag. One of the main mechanisms is strong territoriality, which is exhibited by most large predators.

All non-migratory animals have home ranges, in other words, an area in which they are normally to be found. In non-territorial animals, the home ranges of different individuals or breeding groups overlap. A home range becomes a territory when it is actively defended, in which case the home ranges hardly overlap at all. Territories are usually marked, either with scent patches or by sound signals (such as roaring) or by both.

Lions in the Kruger National Park provide an example of a territorial animal, although the degree of territoriality in lion prides varies. The territory size of a lion pride is relatively fixed in a given environment, although it does vary between different parts of Africa in accordance with the amount of food on offer. In the Kruger National Park, the mean territory size is approximately 10 000 hectares, or ten by ten kilometres. (Incidentally, a territorial lion roar carries about five kilometres, so a male lion can announce his ownership from the middle of the

OPPOSITE, BOTTOM: *Steenbok are usually seen in twos since they are among the few species of antelope that form monogamous pairs. They do not need to drink, as they obtain all the water they need from their food.* RIGHT: *Cheetah*

territory.) The pride, which averages 12 in number in the Kruger National Park, seldom leaves the territory, although it may form sub-groups which split and rejoin amicably. When prides from adjacent territories meet, however, there is usually a fight.

The abutting lion territories more or less fill up the entire landscape, and this places a limit on the total number of lions present. Each pride has one or more adult males of equal rank, several mature females and a number of cubs of different ages. When male cubs reach the age of two or three years and have just learned to hunt for themselves, they are expelled from the pride by the dominant male. They form groups of two to seven 'nomad bachelors'. If there is no empty area for them to move into, they have a very lean time of it for several years, eking out a living in the spaces between existing territories. The mortality rate among these nomad bachelors is very high, but those that survive become strong enough to challenge a dominant male. These challenges are noisy and violent, and are quite unlike the snarls, chases and cuffs that constitute the routine dominance-submission behaviour within the pride. Very often the dominant male or the challenger is killed or seriously hurt.

Once a lion pride is taken over by a new dominant male (or, more frequently, a coalition of males), it is not unusual for all the young cubs sired by the previous dominant males to be killed by the new incumbents. The females then come into oestrus again and are fertilized by the dominant male. In this way, the dominant male ensures that his genes are the ones perpetuated in the pride. There is thus a high degree of relatedness in the pride, which may help to explain, in evolutionary terms, behaviour such as cooperative hunting and feeding.

The behaviour of many herbivore species has evolved to minimize the impact of predation on the continued existence of the population. Impala, for instance, have a breeding system where a single male fertilizes up to 50 females.

LEOPARDS

Leopards kill mainly animals that are small enough to drag up into a tree – this prevents them from being harassed by hyaenas and other scavengers while feeding. Remnants of the carcass may last several days, and will be revisited at night. Carcasses of up to about 100 kilograms have been dragged up trees, illustrating the great strength of these animals. Impala are the most common prey item, followed by bushbuck, reedbuck and waterbuck. The 'average' leopard is thought to kill about 20 times a year. They will take prey as small as a mouse and (occasionally) as large as a wildebeest. Domestic dogs are frequently taken and leopards have been recorded killing and eating jackals. They are probably the major natural enemy of baboons, but a leopard will usually attack only stragglers or at night, since baboons are nearly as large and well-toothed as they are themselves. The combined fury of the troop is sufficient to drive off a leopard during the daytime. Leopards kill their prey by delivering a single bite to the base of the neck.

Leopards are predominantly nocturnal and generally solitary except when mating. Breeding pairs, although they spend little time together, are remarkably faithful to each other. When leopards are seen in groups, the groups are usually made up of a female with her cubs – three is the usual number in a litter. The cubs learn to hunt for themselves at about five months.

The males weigh an average of 60 kilograms, while the female leopards are only half this mass. Both males and females mark out territories with urine, but the male territories tend to be larger and to overlap those of several females.

Although leopards are almost independent of water, they will drink when it is available, and are excellent swimmers. They favour rocky and densely bushed habitat, such as that along rivers. This favours their hunting technique of stalking or ambushing their prey. There is evidence that leopards were major predators of our hominid ancestors.

ABOVE: *There has been some inconclusive debate over whether the female impalas are able to delay giving birth to their young by a week or two, while they await the arrival of the rains. Here a herd of impalas sips in formation at a water hole.*

OPPOSITE, BELOW: *Tawny Eagles are avian predators of guineafowl, francolin, hares, reptiles and amphibians. They have also been known to scavenge, and will steal or 'pirate' the prey of other raptors.*

If one of the females is killed, the herd loses not only that animal but all its future offspring. If one of the superfluous non-breeding males is killed, the long-term impact is close to zero. As a result, unsuccessful males form satellite 'bachelor herds' around the breeding herd, which consists entirely of females, young animals and the dominant male. The brunt of the predation is therefore borne by the bachelor herds.

Herd formation is a widespread phenomenon among the larger antelope. It is believed that the principle advantage is that it reduces the risk of predation. This is sometimes due to mutual defence – for instance, buffalo have been known to attack lions when these predators have been harassing one of their herd, especially if it is a calf, and many a lion has been stunned by a blow from a zebra's hoof. Herd formation is probably due more generally to the advantages of having more eyes, ears and noses available to detect an approaching predator and the confusion which results when an entire herd stampedes off in one thunderous, dusty cloud of thrashing hooves. It is certainly true

RIGHT: *Natal Francolin.* BELOW: *Zebra and wildebeest are often seen together. It has been suggested that the sharp eyesight of the zebra and the excellent sense of smell of the wildebeest form a mutually beneficial combination. The non-ruminant digestive system of zebra equips them to eat coarse grasses, improving the quality of the grassland for species like wildebeest.* OPPOSITE: *Kudus are browsers that feed up to a height of two and a half metres. Since most bushveld trees contain digestion-inhibiting substances, the kudu seldom feeds for more than a minute on a single shrub. The feeding strategy seems to be to select a wide range of plants so that the kudu's detoxifying mechanisms are not overwhelmed by a single type of plant chemical.*

that animals that have become separated from their herds seldom last long, even when they are not sick or injured.

The remarkable synchronization of calving, both within and between species of antelope, is also partly to do with avoiding predation. Many

antelope calve in spring, when the high protein content of the new growth helps females producing milk to suckle their young. Since all the offspring are born in a narrow window of time, the number of lambs is too great for the appetites of waiting predators. The predators become satiated and some lambs survive.

Disease is a special kind of predator, one which has a reproductive rate that is very much faster than that of its prey. This is why diseases typically occur in epidemics which kill a large number of their victims, and then subside again to background levels – as occurred when the rinderpest epidemic ravaged stock and game at the turn of the century. However, even diseases tend not to kill all their hosts. The more resistant host individuals will survive and over a period of time this resistance builds up in the population. This is the reason why indigenous African animals are less susceptible than are introduced cattle to indigenous diseases such as nagana but are very susceptible to the cattle diseases introduced from Europe, such as bovine tuberculosis.

The inherently unstable predator-prey relationships become even more variable when they are played out against a background of fluctuating climate. Grazers can be thought of as predators of grasses, and if the quantity of grass varies between years, grazer numbers must also vary. Rainfall drives grass production, grass production drives grazer numbers, which drive predator numbers. The problem is that all the linkages have some time-lag built into them.

Migration is one way that grazers adapt to seasonal variations in food supply. It is still unclear what role the fence played in the wildebeest population crash of the early 1970s, but it probably contributed to apparent overgrazing which led to the initial culling. After three decades of debate, the fence between Kruger and the adjacent wildlife areas to the west has been removed.

Tourist Facilities on the Central Plains

The central plains region, as befits the richest game-viewing area of the Kruger National Park, is well supplied with tourist accommodation: there are three very popular restcamps, two private camps, two wilderness trails camps and numerous places to picnic or stretch your legs.

Crocodile Bridge is a small camp (58 beds and campsites for 72 people). The camp is adjacent to the Crocodile Bridge Gate. It offers easy access to, and is a good base from which to explore, the rich diversity of the southern landscapes of the Park. There is no restaurant, since this is a relatively small camp.

Lower Sabie Camp is situated 34 kilometres further north and is a deservedly popular camp. It combines an excellent variety of options for guests, including birdwatching and tree identification, as well as game-viewing along the

LEFT AND OPPOSITE, BELOW: *Marabou Storks are usually seen prowling around the feeding frenzies at carcasses. Their straight beak is unsuitable for tearing off meat, so they try to snatch up stray morsels or rob them from other birds. The inflatable neck pouch is used in breeding displays.*
ABOVE: *Tree squirrels can often be seen sunning themselves. Here they catch the early rays of a chilly winter's morning.*

Sabie River with the abundance of animals on the basalt plains. Lower Sabie Camp provides roofed accommodation for 229 visitors and campsites for a further 168.

Satara Camp is the third largest camp in the Park, with beds for 436 and campsites for 360. It is situated towards the north of the region and is said to be the best spot for predators.

Balule Campsite, on the Olifants River in the north of the region, has three six-bedded cottages and campsites for 90 people.

Three three-day, guided wilderness trails on foot are operated out of Metsimetsi, in the Lebombo hills east of Tshokwane; Olifants on the banks of the river with the same name; and Sweni, in the heart of the basalt plains, south-west of Nwanetsi.

RIGHT: *The presence of the Brownheaded Parrot is usually indicated by an ear-piercing whistle. This Lowveld species is found in pairs or flocks of up to ten birds.*
BELOW: *The blood lily* (Ammocharis coranica) *is a bulb that can be found flowering in the Park after the first rains.*

The private camp at Nwanetsi must be taken by a single party of 16 or fewer.

Tshokwane Tearoom, located in the centre of the region, and Nkuhlu Tearoom both offer picnic facilities as well as hot beverages and snacks. The lookout at Orpen Dam is a delightful spot to while away some hours in the shade, overlooking a gorge through the Lebombos. Visitors may also leave their vehicles at Nkumbe, a few kilometres further south; at Mlondozi Dam near Lower Sabie and at Hippo Pool, six kilometres west of Crocodile Bridge.

THE DWARF MONGOOSE

There are eight species of mongoose in the Kruger National Park. Dwarf mongooses are diurnal and are often seen as they move around their territories in bands that usually number between ten and twenty but can include up to fifty individuals. These small mammals have a home range of about ten hectares. The dominant female has a particularly well-developed sense of geography: she will follow an almost predictable path between her safe overnight haven (usually in a termite mound) and the band's midday siesta spots. She then leads the band on to the next sleeping place, covering several hundred metres a day and returning to the starting point after a week or two.

The mongoose band is never more than the sentry's alarm call away from a known bolt-hole. The band forages only for about five hours a day – two and a half hours in the morning and the same amount of time in the late afternoon. Much of the rest of the day is spent sleeping or in social behaviour such as playing and mutual grooming. If the humble mongoose can make a living in a very harsh environment by working just five hours a day, it is unclear why our advanced technology can't allow us to do the same.

(Reference: Rasa, A. Mongoose Watch.*)*

THE LEBOMBOS

THE LANDSCAPE ALONG THE EASTERN BORDER

In the wildlife areas of Africa many less spectacular but equally interesting organisms are missed in the hunt for the 'big five'. The Lebombo hills, which form the eastern boundary of the Park, contain many of these overlooked treasures.

There is a good reason for the relative scarcity of large mammals in the Lebombos. The hills are composed of rhyolite, a form of lava that originates from relatively close to the surface of the molten magma and is thus rich in silica but poor in basic cations. As a result it is hard and very resistant to weathering. This is why the Lebombos stand as a ridge above the surrounding basalt plains. The soil erodes from the slopes of the Lebombos nearly as fast as it forms, so it is not only inherently rather poor but it is also very thin and stony. The grasses that grow on it are sour and unproductive, and thus are able to support only a low density of herbivores. The dominant tree in this area is the red bushwillow (*Combretum apiculatum*), again indicating the relative infertility of the soil. The Lebombos form an isolated area of higher elevation and rainfall stretching from the Kruger Park southwards through Swaziland to northern KwaZulu-Natal.

ABOVE: *Vervet monkeys.* LEFT: *African wild cats are genetically the same species as domestic cats. Potential interbreeding is the reason Park staff may not keep cats as pets.* RIGHT: *Typical rhyolite boulders in the Lebombo hills.*

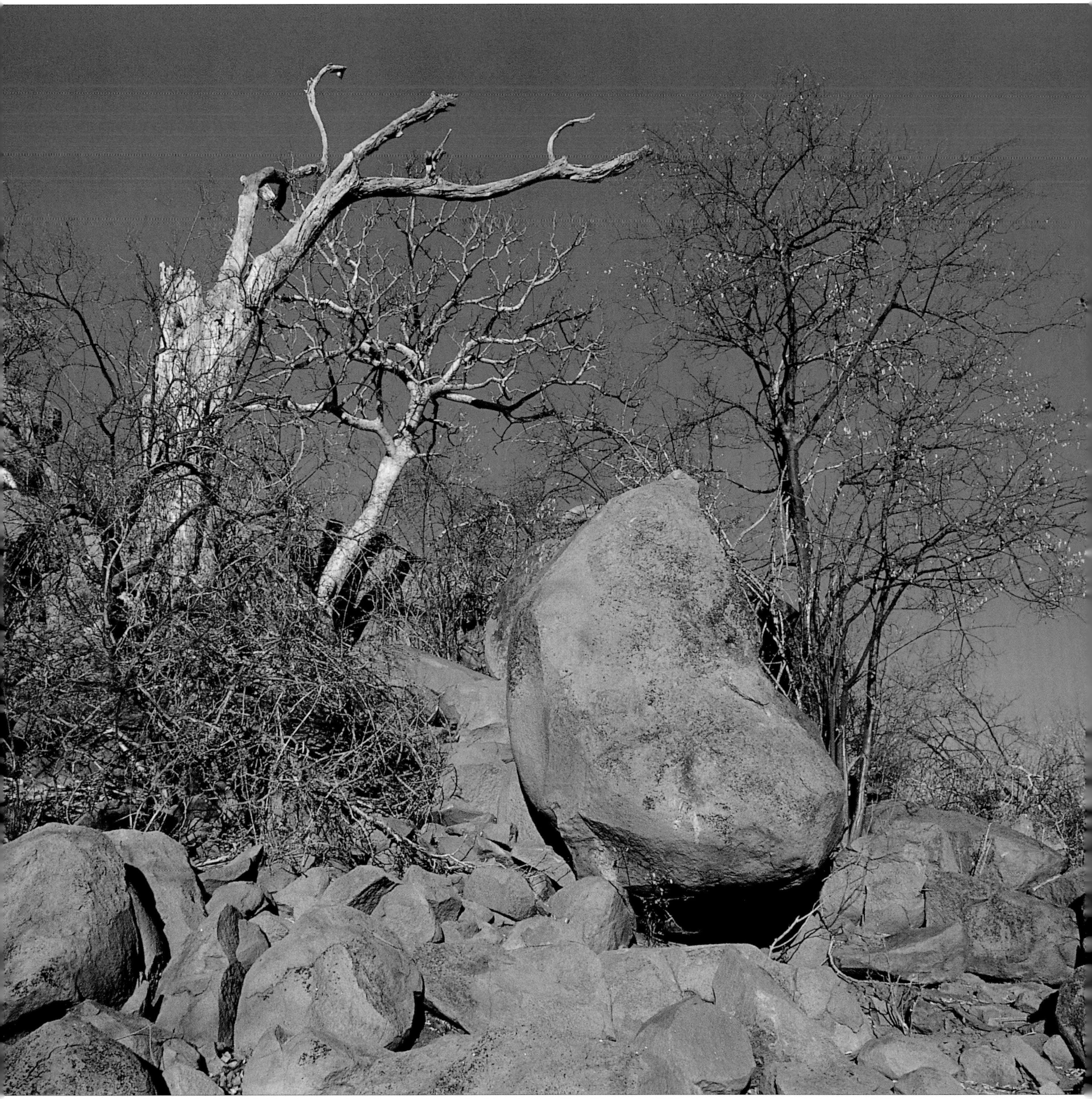

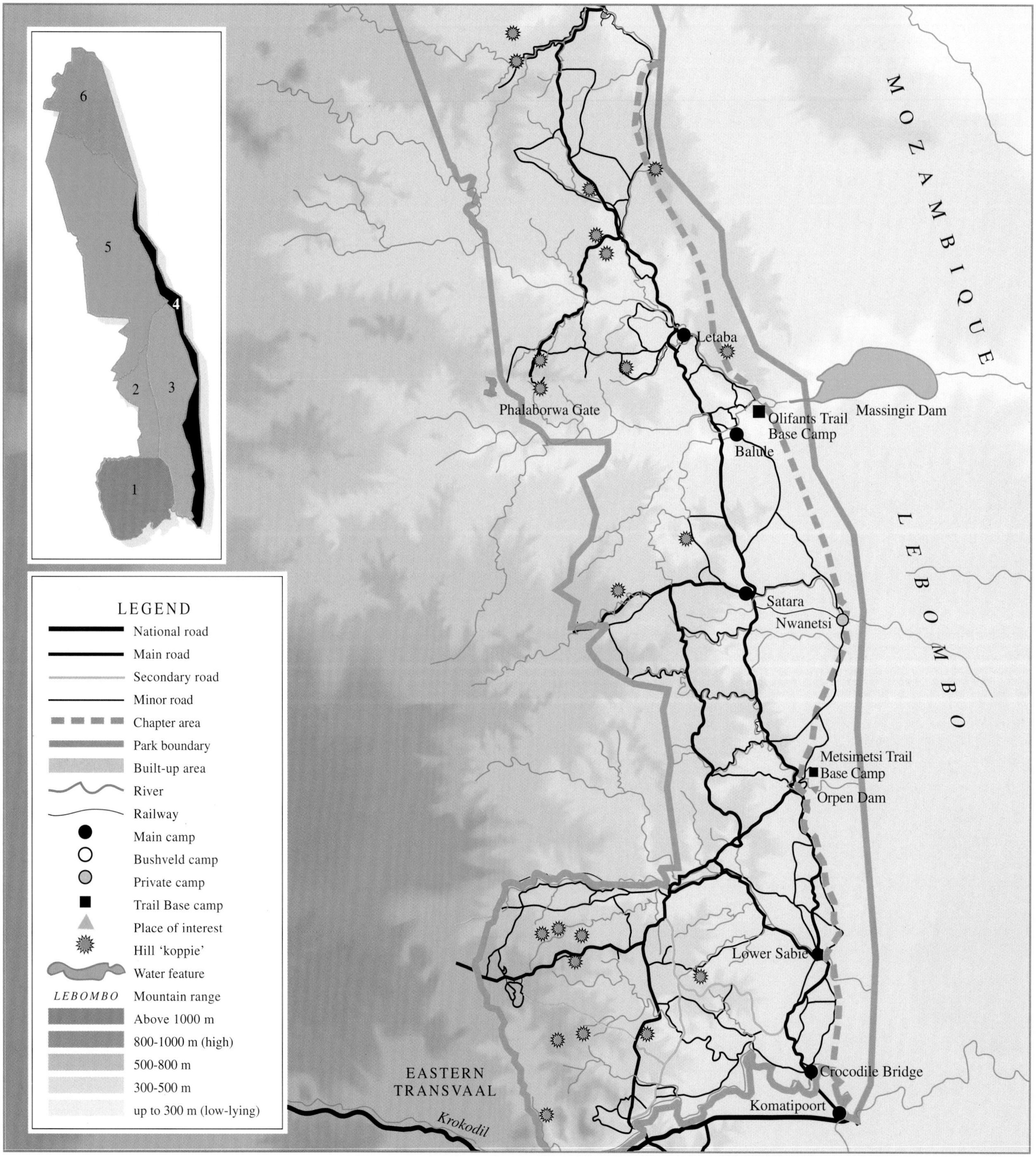
6
5
4
2
3
1
LEGEND
National road
Main road
Secondary road
Minor road
Chapter area
Park boundary
Built-up area
River
Railway
Main camp
Bushveld camp
Private camp
Trail Base camp
Place of interest
Hill 'koppie'
Water feature
LEBOMBO Mountain range
Above 1000 m
800-1000 m (high)
500-800 m
300-500 m
up to 300 m (low-lying)
MOZAMBIQUE
Letaba
Phalaborwa Gate
Olifants Trail
Base Camp
Massingir Dam
Balule
LEBOMBO
Satara
Nwanetsi
Metsimetsi Trail
Base Camp
Orpen Dam
Lower Sabie
Crocodile Bridge
Komatipoort
EASTERN
TRANSVAAL
Krokodil

They are well known for the botanical rarities they harbour, such as euphorbias, some of which occur only in or around the Park: *Euphorbia evansii* is confined mainly to the Kruger Park.

When ecologists are confronted by a large number of apparently similar organisms inhabiting the same space, one of the first questions to occur to them, is how these species divide up the available resources in order to coexist.

In general, coexisting species will either use slightly different parts of the resource, or they will utilize the resource at different times. An example of this is the separation in feeding heights among browsers. What is notable in this and in other examples of niche separation is less the separation than the high degree of overlap of niches that can be tolerated. In fact, although in theory competitors should exclude one another, in practice it can be seen that the natural world is full of apparent competitors which coexist quite happily.

RIGHT: *Klipspringers are usually found in pairs or small family groups. They are very agile in moving across rocky terrain and up steep, rock-covered slopes, hence their common name, meaning 'rock jumper' in Afrikaans.*

One of the reasons why competition is not the powerful force in shaping animal communities that it has sometimes been depicted as, is that competition is seldom a steady, continuous process. For most of the time, the resource that the organisms share is not scarce, so the overlapping needs are not in conflict. Only during the occasional periods of resource shortage does separation become important. Competition may therefore occasionally be intense, but it is generally quite lax.

There is a great variety of small predators in the Kruger Park, most of which are nocturnal. The proportion of their diet consisting of small

LEBOMBO EUPHORBIA

*The Lebombo euphorbia (*Euphorbia confinalis *subsp.* confinalis*) is a rare succulent tree found in the Park. 'Confinalis' in the species' name refers to the fact that its distribution broadly coincides with the international border between South Africa and neighbouring countries. Biologists prefer to use the term 'endemic' for plants that are restricted to a given area rather than the vague term 'indigenous'. Since plants and animals pay scant attention to national boundaries, to classify an organism as indigenous to South Africa has little biological meaning.*

Like most euphorbias, this species and Euphorbia evansii *have a poisonous milky sap. It is extremely irritating if it finds its way into sensitive places such as the eyes, and should be washed out immediately. The poisonous sap of the euphorbias is the major reason for the folklore that wild fruits with milky sap should be avoided; if this advice were followed a large proportion of the edible and tasty wild fruits would be eliminated as well. The sap of euphorbias also contains a latex which was once investigated as a substitute for rubber.*

Although euphorbias bear a striking resemblance to the cacti of north and central America, they are in no way related. The similarity is merely a striking example of how plants that live in different areas but are faced with similar environments evolve similar growth forms. In this case the challenge of aridity has resulted in the loss of leaves, with the stems becoming green and photosynthetic in their place. Since stems have a larger internal volume per unit of surface area than leaves, this adaptation helps the plants to conserve water.

The genus Euphorbia *is part of a family known as the Euphorbiaceae that includes plants as diverse as a tiny succulent and a towering tree. As in all plant families, the unifying factor lies in the design of the flower; in the case of the Euphorbiaceae, the female parts of the flower have three chambers and are raised on a short stalk.*

BELOW: *The conspicuous red throat and face and the large, black, decurved bill identify the Ground Hornbill, a predator of tortoises.*
OPPOSITE: *Enormous, old baobabs (*Adansonia digitata*) are very slow-growing; carbon dating of larger specimens has shown them to be over a thousand years old. Baobabs bear leaves only briefly, and have white flowers – thought to be pollinated by bats. The woody fruits contain black seeds in a dry white pulp which is acidic but refreshing to suck.*

mammals varies from an almost exclusive food source to an occasional snack. The caracal with its distinctive ear-tufts is large enough to kill a small antelope, but its diet is dominated by birds, hares and rodents.

The serval is slightly smaller (about the size of a very large domestic cat, and built and marked rather like a small cheetah). It is too lightly built to regularly kill even small antelope, and lives mainly on rodents and birds.

Many of the features of African wild cats – the tall stance imparted by long front legs and the distinctive reddish ears – can be observed in domestic and semi-wild cats of the Lowveld because African wild cats and domestic cats interbreed freely. The Park staff actively exterminate cross-bred cats within the Kruger Park lest the wild race become diluted with genes from other sources. In truth, there are so many cats on the fringes of the Park that it is doubtful if any pure-bred African wild cats exist in the Kruger Park any longer. This example raises a difficult question: what constitutes the conservation of biodiversity? Should conservationists concentrate on saving the gene, the population, the species or a whole community of species? If conservation were

regarded as a matter of preserving only the African wild cat genes, then this aim would be equally well served by allowing the genes to be preserved in the domestic cat population. Conservationists usually argue that a certain subset of genes, which result in a distinct appearance or behaviour in a subpopulation associated with a particular environment, are worthy of conservation in their own right. They further argue that the best place to achieve that

OPPOSITE, TOP: *The wood of the Lebombo iron-wood (*Androstachys johnsonii*) is so hard it was once used as nails.* OPPOSITE, BELOW: *The red-leaved rock fig (*Ficus ingens*) belongs to a group of figs known as rock splitters – typically found clinging to boulders; the Night Adder is a mildly venomous snake.* RIGHT: *The Gymnogene clambers around on trees, looking into crevices.*

conservation is in the environment that gave rise to the adaptations, where gene-environment interactions can reinforce each other.

If it is accepted that genetic variation at a level below that of the full species should be specially protected, what about curiosities such as the 'white lions' that periodically appear in Kruger prides, as a result of a mutation in one of the genes for coat pigmentation? The 'king cheetahs', which have large amalgamated black patches rather than the discrete splotches of ordinary cheetahs, are in the same category. Are they something special, or just freaks?

The concept of a 'race' is rather poorly defined biologically. A species consists of all organisms able to interbreed and produce fertile offspring: the features which distinguish one race from another are not important enough to the animal itself to stand in the way of reproduction. A subspecies, on the other hand, does have a breeding barrier. This rank is usually reserved for populations which could potentially interbreed but are prevented from doing so by geographical separation. Where that separation has existed for a long period of time, the different populations have usually diverged sufficiently to be visually distinct; for example, the several giraffe subspecies in Africa have distinctive coat patterns.

There are eight species of mongoose in the Kruger Park. Most are nocturnal but the two social species (the dwarf mongoose and banded mongoose) are diurnal and often seen. In dwarf mongoose bands, one or two individuals are always on guard against raptors, their main enemy. These sentinels are continuously changed, in a very orderly way, as the band moves along on its foraging path. By keeping guard, the sentinel reduces risk to others but exposes itself to greater danger. If evolution is the selfish process of maximizing the survival of one's own genes, why are the genes for such

altruistic behaviour not swiftly eliminated? In the case of the dwarf mongoose this paradox has been resolved: all the members of a band are genetically highly related, so saving another member of the band is equivalent to saving oneself. This situation comes about through a system of social organization. The dominant animal in a band is a fertile female, who suppresses the fertility of all other females in the band by a combination of behavioural and hormonal control. The dominant female mates with only one male, so all the offspring are siblings.

Porcupines are rarely seen during the daylight, although evidence of their presence is common; shed quills can frequently be seen along the roads. Most of these quills are not lost through conflict with predators but in defending the territory against other porcupines. It seems that the Park road system often defines the boundaries between territories. Despite their spiny armour, porcupines are the favourite prey of lions, especially old lions that no longer belong to a pride and lack the speed and strength to hunt large animals. Porcupines do not shoot their quills at attackers, as is sometimes believed, but reverse into their attacker with raised quills. Lions punctured in this way are usually able to pull the quills out, either themselves or with the help of another member of the pride during grooming sessions.

The Kruger Park is home to two species of galago. As the Afrikaans name for the lesser galago implies, they are nocturnal primates ('nagapie' means 'night-ape'). Although lesser galagos are widespread in the savannas of southern Africa, they are infrequently seen during daytime. They emerge from their communal nests in hollow trees towards twilight to play with and groom each other before setting out to forage individually. Lesser galagos eat mostly the gum of trees but are also partial to insects.

Like most animals that rely on their night vision, the retina in the galago's eyes is backed by a reflective layer. This causes the photons of

LEFT: *The leaves of the red-leaved rock fig are a translucent pinkish colour for a few days in the springtime.* ABOVE AND BELOW: *Play forms an important part of the daily lives of young chacma baboons.*

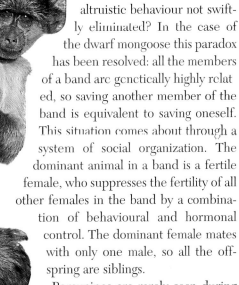

ABOVE: *Mutual grooming has a social function and also rids the animals of pests.*
RIGHT: *The grey duiker is one of the most widespread small antelopes in Africa. It is a browser that is able to survive in the generally unpalatable broad-leaved savannas due to its ability to pick out the higher-quality forage: fallen fruit makes up a large part of its diet at some times of the year.* OPPOSITE, LEFT: *A young baboon.* OPPOSITE, BELOW: *Martial Eagle.*

light to be detectable both on their way into the retina and on their way out of it. In the beam of a headlamp or a torch the eyes of the galago shine back at the observer like a pair of brilliant rubies. Galagos seldom leave the canopies of trees, making spectacular leaps from one canopy to another. They mark their territory by

urinating on their hands – the major drawback of what would otherwise be a delightful pet. It has been claimed that the purpose of this behaviour is to improve its grip as the galago leaps from branch to branch.

The thick-tailed galago is larger than the lesser galago and is confined to riverine forests. It is seldom seen but its blood-curdling human-like screams (from which it gets the common name 'bush baby') can sometimes be heard at night. It is quite common around Skukuza Camp.

Apart from galagos and our own species, there are three other species of primate in the Kruger Park: the chacma baboon, the vervet monkey and the samango monkey. The last-named is confined to the riverine forest in the Pafuri region, where it was reintroduced in recent years following local extinction. Vervet monkeys are widespread in the savanna regions of southern Africa. They live in troops of 15 to 20, which often join amicably with other troops while feeding, splitting up again in the evening.

The social organization of troops of chacma baboons has been extensively studied by primatologists. The many-talented South African writer and naturalist Eugene Marais was far ahead of his time when he studied a troop of baboons in the Waterberg mountains by living among them for months at a time, describing his observations in the classic books *My Friends the Baboons* and *Soul of the Ape*. That technique has subsequently been applied with great success to gorillas, chimpanzees and orang-utans. The baboon troops in the Kruger Park can contain up to 100 individuals. When two troops meet there is usually little aggression unless they are both

ABOVE: *The tree squirrel occurs widely in the Kruger National Park. It is usually seen singly or in small groups consisting of a mother and young. It lives, however, in loose association with other members of its species.* ABOVE, RIGHT: *Diederick Cuckoos have a wide range of hosts including weavers and sparrows, but their eggs, when laid, tend to match those of the host birds.* RIGHT: *Young spotted hyaenas play-fighting in the grass.* OPPOSITE: *The black-backed jackal is mainly nocturnal in agricultural areas but in protected reserves it is frequently seen during the day. Pairs form a long-term bond, with both the male and female defending their territory.*

aiming to use the same favourite sleeping spot. The troops are led by dominant males, which can weigh up to 43 kilograms. When several adult males gang up they present a fearsome array of teeth, and have been known to put lions to flight. The dominance hierarchy among the males is maintained by continuous small acts of threat and submission, which only occasionally break out into open fights. Cohesion in the troop, on the other hand, is nurtured by grooming, mostly of males and infants by the females. The male baboons generally return the favour only when the female is fertile, which is advertised by the swollen and coloured skin around her genitalia.

There are about 150 troops of baboons in the Kruger Park. Each occupies a home range of between 13 and 23 square kilometres. The troop moves two to 15 kilometres in a day, foraging as it goes. Baboons will eat virtually anything. The bulk of their diet consists of the swollen part at the base of grass tufts and the thickened roots of grasses, known as rhizomes. Both of these organs store sugars and starches; like humans, baboons are unable to digest the

Bats

The mammal group with the most species in the Kruger Park is bats. There are 41 species and possibly some still unaccounted for. Compare this, for instance, with the species of antelopes (22) or those in the cat family (6).

The two main feeding groups of bats are the fruit-eaters and the insect-eaters. Further differences between the species have to do with the type and size of insects and fruit eaten, and in the choice of roosting sites.

*The flowers of some trees are pollinated by bats, such as the baobab (*Adansonia digitata*) and the sausage tree (*Kigelia africana*).*

The structures of the nose and ears of many species are part of the mechanisms that allow them to navigate in total darkness[23].

Right: Epauletted fruitbat

cellulose which makes up the bulk of the grass. Baboons overturn stones in search of scorpions and insects, and they also kill and eat young birds, hares or even small antelope that they find hiding in the grass.

On a plateau of the Lebombos, midway between Nwanetsi and the Olifant River gorges, is an area known as the Pumbe sandveld that contains some unexpected riches. Not only are the plants that grow here rather different from the species of the surrounding landscape, but a series of small, ephemeral pans found in the sandveld contains two endemic fish species with a fascinating lifecycle. One of them is probably the rarest fish in South Africa: the total world population is probably no more than a few hundred individuals. Both killifish species must hatch from eggs laid in the dry mud, grow, breed and lay eggs again before the pans dry out. Perhaps because of the urgency of their task, the male fish is brilliantly coloured.

The Kruger National Park includes, at last count, 53 species of what could loosely be called lizards. Biologists divide these up into five main groups. Geckos, with their sucker-like fingers, are the well-known, friendly creatures that dart around the bungalow walls at night, eating insects; there are 14 species in the Kruger National Park, most attractively spotted. The smooth-skinned, agile reptiles, mostly longitudinally striped and often seen sunning themselves on rocks, are properly called skinks; there are 13 skink species, several of which are legless, and could easily be mistaken for snakes. Also snake-like are the rarely seen amphisbaenians (six species), which live under stones or logs, or in sandy soils. There are 19 species of true lizard, the scaly, prehistoric-looking creatures rather like miniature dragons; true lizards include the three species of agama, which have large (sometimes brightly coloured) heads and flattened bodies, and are often seen on rocks or tree bark. The chameleon (one species) is hard to describe but probably needs no introduction: who has not marvelled at a picture of these colour-changing creatures with their long sticky tongues and independent eyes?

The Kruger Park also has a rich diversity of snakes: 54 species at last count. Of these, only nine (members of the cobra and the adder families) are highly poisonous. A further four or so are equally poisonous but the poison fangs are at the back of the mouth, so fatal bites to a victim the size of a human are rare. The largest number of species kill their prey by constriction; of these, only the African python grows large enough to be of danger to humans. If you see a snake the chances are, therefore, that it is harmless. Observe it from a safe distance and admire its beauty and design.

LEFT: *There are eight species of mongoose in the Kruger National Park. Pictured here is the dwarf mongoose.*
OPPOSITE: *Sharpe's grysbok is a small browser, usually found in hilly habitats. It could easily be confused with the much commoner steenbok but Sharpe's grysbok can be distinguished by its reddish coat flecked with occasional grey hairs, while the steenbok shows a white rump and dark ear-veins.*

The difference between turtles, tortoises and terrapins varies according to what part of the world you come from. In South Africa, the word 'turtle' is reserved for marine species. The freshwater species with low-domed shells are called terrapins (there are three species in the Kruger Park), and the truly terrestrial, high-domed species are tortoises (three species occur in the Park). Tortoises lay their eggs underground during the spring but the eggs only hatch the following summer, thus avoiding the dry-season fires which kill many of the adults; they are also killed by a wide range of predators, from hyaenas to hornbills.

Terrapins can be found in most standing water in the Kruger National Park, and in the small, temporary pans. They are carnivores and their diet includes frogs, snails and even careless birds. If handled, terrapins produce a powerful and penetrating odour which has been said to resemble the smell of lions. Crocodiles are their principal predator.

Tourist Facilities in the Lebombos

There are no restcamps and few roads in this hilly region. The Metsimetsi Wilderness Trail Camp is the only accommodation in the Lebombo hills; Olifants Wilderness Trail Camp is on the edge. There is a picnic site and private camp at Nwanetsi, on the lower slopes of the Lebombos. The game-viewing hide at Orpen Dam overlooks a rocky gorge where the N'waswitsonto River carves its way through the hills.

RIVERS AND WATER HOLES

THE VEINS OF THE LANDSCAPE

Rivers bring life to the land. They also drain the waste products of the upstream organs to the sump of the ocean. In the case of the rivers that flow through the Kruger Park, they are bled almost dry before they reach the Park boundary.

The Olifants River is one of only four perennial rivers that flow through the Park, and has the largest catchment of any river in the region. The headwaters are in the industrial heartland of South Africa, the coal-rich Eastern Transvaal Highveld. When coal is exposed to oxygen and water in an abandoned open-cast mine or an unrehabilitated spoils dump, the sulphur in the coal forms sulphuric acid which seeps into the groundwater and then into the rivers.

The Olifants flows northwards, picking up the waste products of the metallurgical industry, and enters the Loskop Dam, one of many impoundments between its source and the sea. Here water is drawn off for the irrigation of farms. The excess drains back to the river, carrying with it salts, fertilisers and pesticide residues. The river then curves in a great arc eastwards. For most of this reach it flows through

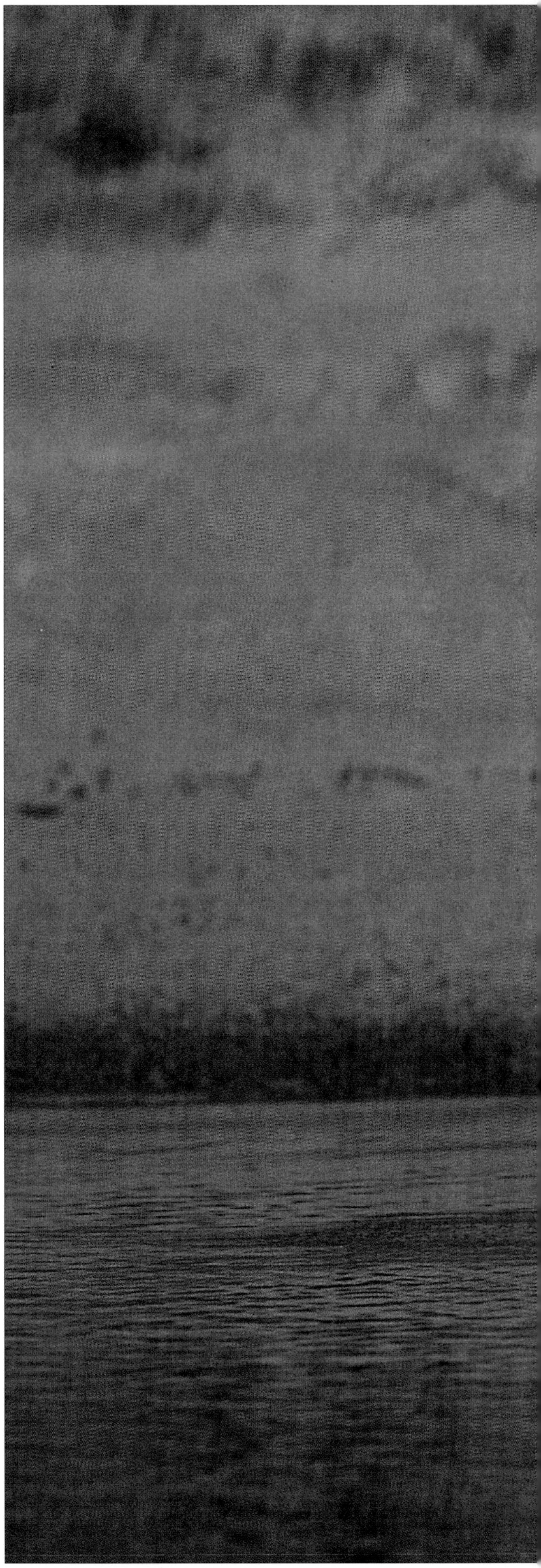

TOP: *Rivers and water holes are a paradise for waterbird lovers.* LEFT: *Impala.* RIGHT: *Animals vary in their water requirements: waterbuck are seldom found far from water since they need to drink daily; small browsers do not need to drink at all.*

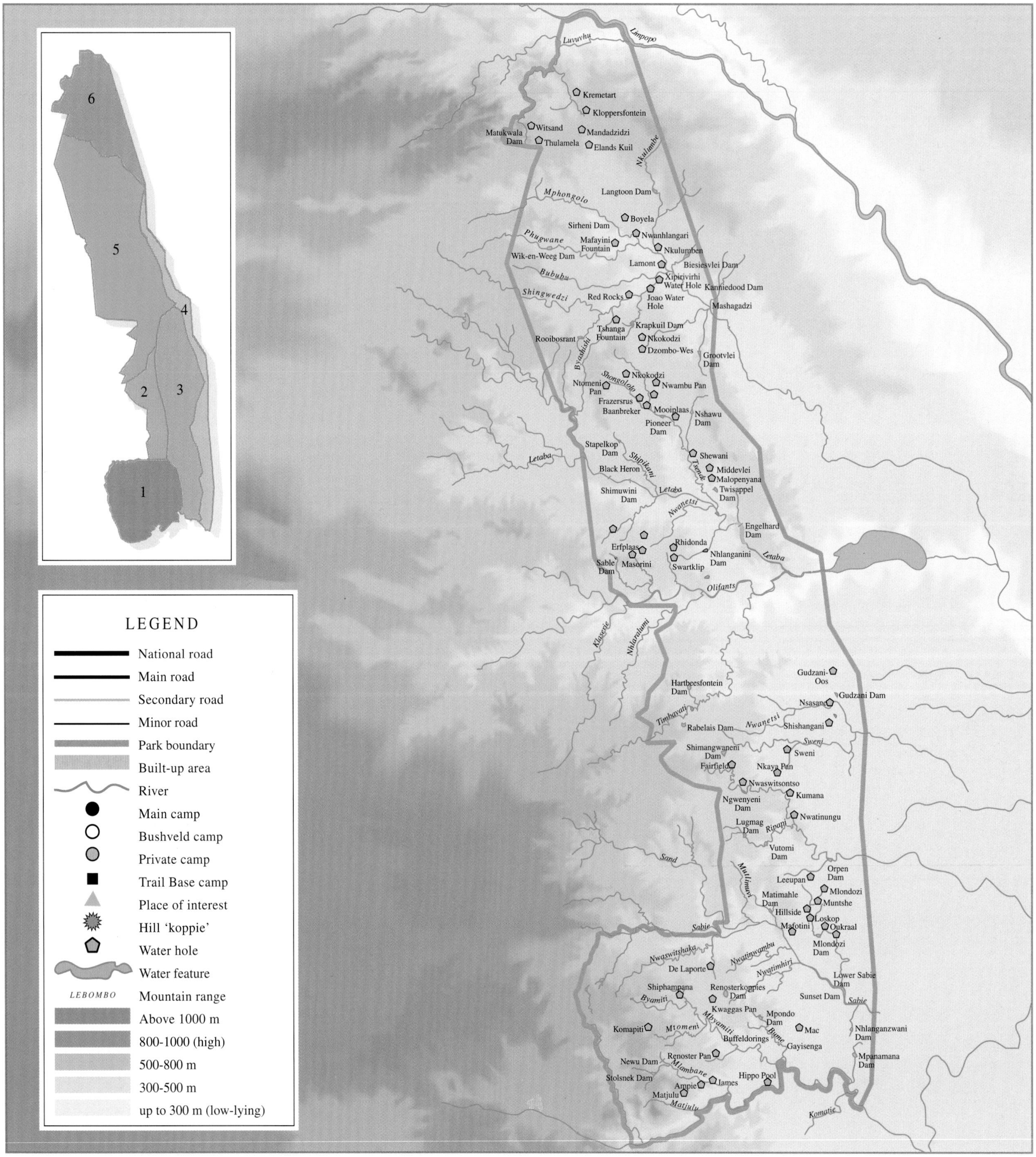
6
5
4
2
3
1
LEGEND
National road
Main road
Secondary road
Minor road
Park boundary
Built-up area
River
Main camp
Bushveld camp
Private camp
Trail Base camp
Place of interest
Hill 'koppie'
Water hole
Water feature
LEBOMBO
Mountain range
Above 1000 m
800-1000 (high)
500-800 m
300-500 m
up to 300 m (low-lying)
Luvuvhu
Limpopo
Kremetart
Kloppersfontein
Matukwala Dam
Witsand
Mandadzidzi
Thulamela
Elands Kuil
Nkulumbe
Mphongolo
Langtoon Dam
Boyela
Sirheni Dam
Nwanhlangari
Phugwane
Mafayini Fountain
Nkulumbeni
Wik-en-Weeg Dam
Lamont
Biesiesvlei Dam
Bububu
Xipirivirhi Water Hole
Kanniedood Dam
Shingwedzi
Red Rocks
Joao Water Hole
Mashagadzi
Tshanga Fountain
Krapkuil Dam
Rooibosrant
Nkokodzi
Dzombo-Wes
Grootvlei Dam
Nkokodzi
Nwambu Pan
Ntomeni Pan
Shongololo
Frazersrus
Baanbreker
Mooiplaas
Nshawu Dam
Pioneer Dam
Stapelkop Dam
Letaba
Shipikani
Shewani
Black Heron
Tsende
Middevlei
Malopenyana
Shimuwini Dam
Letaba
Twisappel Dam
Nwanetsi
Engelhard Dam
Rhidonda
Erfplaas
Nhlanganini Dam
Letaba
Sable Dam
Masorini
Swartklip
Olifants
Klaserie
Nhlaralumi
Gudzani-Oos
Hartbeesfontein Dam
Gudzani Dam
Nsasane
Timbavati
Rabelais Dam
Nwanetsi
Shishangani
Sweni
Shimangwaneni Dam
Sweni
Fairfield
Nkaya Pan
Nwaswitsontso
Kumana
Ngwenyeni Dam
Nwatinungu
Lugmag Dam
Ripape
Vutomi Dam
Sand
Mutlumuvi
Orpen Dam
Leeupan
Mlondozi
Matimahle Dam
Muntshe
Hillside
Loskop
Mafotini
Oukraal
Sabie
Mlondozi Dam
Nwaswitshaka
Nwatimwambu
De Laporte
Nwatimhiri
Lower Sabie Dam
Shiphampana
Renosterkoppies Dam
Sunset Dam
Sabie
Byamiti
Kwaggas Pan
Mpondo Dam
Komapiti
Mtomeni
Mbyamiti
Mac
Nhlanganzwani Dam
Buffeldorings
Biyamiti
Gayisenga
Renoster Pan
Newu Dam
Mpanamana Dam
Mlambane
Hippo Pool
Stolsnek Dam
Ampie
James
Matjulu
Matjulu
Komatie

tribal communal lands and silt from the over-grazed landscape is added to the load in the river. The Steelpoort River, which joins the Olifants, drains the eastern edge of the Bushveld Igneous Complex, source of rare and valuable metals such as chromium, platinum, palladium and rhodium. Unfortunately, these 'heavy metals' are also very toxic.

Just before it enters the Kruger Park, the Olifants flows past the mines at Phalaborwa. By the time it enters the Kruger Park just east of Phalaborwa, the Olifants River is a toxic trickle. For significant periods of the year, the concentrations of fluoride, chloride and phosphate greatly exceed the guidelines for human and animal consumption. The floods which could scour the river system of pollutants are tamed by the string of dams in the headwaters so the water is turbid with algae and silt. (The water supply for the Olifants and Balule camps, incidentally, is purified.)

Sycamore Fig

The stately fig trees that line the banks of Lowveld rivers are mostly sycamore fig trees (Ficus sycamorus). *These trees have a characteristic yellowish bark that peels off in fine, papery flakes. The fruits are borne in clusters, directly on the main stem of the tree – a common feature among lowland forest trees, along with the spreading buttress roots that many possess.*

The figs are edible but not very palatable in southern Africa, due to their infestation by dozens of tiny, symbiotic wasps. Fig fruits can be thought of as mulberries turned inside out – the wasps are responsible for fertilizing the flowers which, since they are completely enclosed by the fruit, are never exposed to other pollinators. Eggs are laid in the young fig by a female wasp. The male wasps are completely wingless and spend their entire lives in the fruit. The females escape via the small opening at the top of the fig, which is surrounded by male flowers. Laden with pollen, they proceed to another fig, fertilizing it in the process. Each fig species has its own dedicated wasp species – a fine example of the interdependency of nature.

The sycamore fig is grown as a fruit tree in the Middle East (it is the tree that Zacchius is said to have climbed to observe the arrival of Christ in Jerusalem). Since the wasps do not extend that far north, the figs are edible but rely on humans to be fertilized. Baboons, monkeys and birds relish the fruits and the tree canopy is usually alive with activity.

Despite this gloomy situation, the river supports one of the major hippo populations in the Park and ten pairs of Pel's Fishing Owls – as many as the Luvuvhu River, which is generally regarded as the prime place in South Africa to spot these rare birds.

The mandate of the Kruger National Park is to conserve all forms of nature within its boundaries, including the invertebrates, fish and amphibians in its rivers, the riparian vegetation and the water-birds. This is a near-impossible task when both the quality and quantity of the water entering the Park is outside the control of the Park authorities. Water is the factor most limiting development throughout South Africa. It is difficult to argue the needs and rights of caddis-flies and catfish when a large part of the human population has no access to clean water.

Furthermore, upliftment of people needs a strong economy, and an economy built on mines and industry needs water. Farming is another way to turn water into wealth, albeit with a lower efficiency than industry, and farmers argue that they provide essential food and jobs. Clearly there are merits to all the water claims; but cleaning up the rivers and using the water as sparingly and fairly as possible will obviously be to everyone's benefit.

The first step towards addressing these problems is the recognition that rivers cannot be managed piecemeal. Decisions need to be made within the context of the entire catchment area. The catchment management approach is increasingly being adopted in South Africa, but in a catchment area the size of the Olifants River, draining three political regions and two countries, this is difficult to achieve.

The second step is to recognize that riparian ecosystems, which consists of all those organisms

OPPOSITE: *Male hippos are aggressively territorial. While generally placid away from the river, they will instinctively bite if startled or cornered. Several tourists (although none in the Kruger Park) have died after advancing too close on foot to an apparently placid hippo.*
ABOVE AND RIGHT: *The diet of crocodiles consists mostly of the large catfish ('barbel') and terrapins which live in all the rivers, pans and dams of the Kruger National Park. They also snatch unwary antelope and at night venture long distances to scavenge on carcasses.*

dependent on the river, are legitimate water users, with rights equal to other users. They support a complex web of life, and in the process partially purify the water. These ecosystems are now considered to be valid water users under South African law, but this is a relatively recent view, and most of the water rights have already been allocated. A good start in determining the minimum needs of an ecosystem is to launch a research effort, such as the Kruger Park Rivers Programme.

River-bank plants need a continuous supply of water. While the trees of the savannas tolerate a drought of several months' duration every year, a similar drought would kill the stately trees of riparian forests. This is true for the many rivers in the Kruger Park that are apparently dry for most of the year: below the surface of the sand, water is flowing. Rough calculations can be made of the amount of water needed in order to maintain transpiration by the riparian vegetation. Since the rivers are a ribbon-like oasis within the parched landscape, evaporative demand on riparian plants is high. They are 'thirstier' than their dryland counterparts because they have not needed to evolve mechanisms for conserving water. For a large Kruger Park river, say ten metres wide with riparian forests 50 metres wide on either side, the evaporation could add up to 300 million litres per kilometre of river length per year. This is enough water to supply 40 000 rural people with their basic minimum of 25 litres a day but it is only a small proportion of the total flow of water in the river.

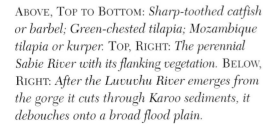

ABOVE, TOP TO BOTTOM: *Sharp-toothed catfish or barbel; Green-chested tilapia; Mozambique tilapia or kurper.* TOP, RIGHT: *The perennial Sabie River with its flanking vegetation.* BELOW, RIGHT: *After the Luvuvhu River emerges from the gorge it cuts through Karoo sediments, it debouches onto a broad flood plain.*

Rivers, perhaps even more than other ecosystems, are dependent on disturbances to maintain their vitality. Floods scour away sediment that clogs up the pools and deposit fertile silt on the flood plains. By washing away portions of riverine vegetation they restart the succession of plant communities which provides the diversity of the riverine habitat.

Floods have become rarer and smaller with the building of dams and the changes in land use in the upper catchment. The challenge to ecologists and engineers is to work out how frequent and how large these floods should be, and to design and operate the dams to simulate a natural flooding regime, while still satisfying their other objectives.

The headwaters of many Lowveld rivers are located in the mountains of the escarpment west of the Park. The last fifty years have seen three quarters of the natural montane grasslands disappear under plantations of pine and eucalyptus trees. In a land where only 0,02 per cent of the surface area is covered by natural forests, the plantations are essential to meet the national needs for timber and paper. However, only about five per cent of South Africa is climatically suitable for growing timber – and much of that area falls in the catchment area of the Kruger National Park. One of the hidden costs of the industry is the impact it has on the rivers of the Lowveld.

Although trees and grasses have a fairly similar maximum rate of water use, trees are able to extract water from the soil for a longer period. The deep rooting systems of eucalyptus trees, in particular, allow them to continue drawing water during the dry season, when the grasses would be dormant. This water is then not available to maintain the steady base flow in the rivers during the dry season.

The planting of new forests is tightly regulated by law. The forestry companies may plant only up to a given fraction of the land in a catchment. They may not plant exotic timber trees within ten metres of a stream, nor may they remove indigenous forest to replace it with plantations. When the plantation forests are felled, large patches of disturbed ground are exposed to the elements until a new plantation cover can be established. Since some of the forests are planted on very steep lands, this exposed soil is prone to erosion. The strips of undisturbed riparian vegetation help to keep the silt out of the rivers.

Both the forest industry and the quality of water in the rivers face a threat in the form of 'acid rain'. Nearly 140 million tons of coal are consumed in South Africa every year, most of it in a relatively small area between the Pretoria-Johannesburg-Vereeniging metropolis and the coalfields around Witbank. The sulphur in this coal is injected into the atmosphere as a gas and carried southwards and eastwards, towards the Indian Ocean. On the way it is transformed into sulphuric acid, some of which falls on the Kruger Park and in the catchment areas of the rivers that feed it.

Only about one quarter of the acid fall-out occurs in rainwater – the majority descends as dust-like, dry, crystal particles. If this fall-out continues at high rates and for long periods of time, however, the acid will overwhelm the natural buffering capacity of the soil. Essential

BELOW: *Aptly known as 'the lone grey fisherman', the Grey Heron hunts solitarily along the margins of most expanses of water in the Park. Its diet consists mainly of fish.*

plant nutrients will be acid-leached out of the soil, polluting the rivers and leading to deficiencies in the plants.

Acid deposition is not new to the Lowveld. The rainfall there is naturally acidic, partly due to the sulphur and nitrogen gases released from vegetation fires. Several research projects are currently underway to determine the seriousness of the threat of acid deposition. The plants and soils of the Lowveld are probably quite resistant to the slow input of acid, because the soils have a relatively high buffering capacity. Some of the soils of the escarpment, on the other hand, are strongly acidic to start off with and have a low capacity to absorb further acid. Furthermore, pine trees are especially sensitive to acid deposition.

Experience gained from other parts of the world suggests that the ecosystems in South Africa can tolerate only one or two more decades of acid deposition. After that serious problems will begin to appear.

LEFT: *Burchell's zebra are dependent on water and are seldom found more than ten kilometres away from it.* BELOW: *Elephants dig for water in sandy, dry river beds and other animals subsequently benefit from this water source.*

The annual rainfall in the Lowveld is so variable that the concept of an expected amount of rain is not very useful – very few years actually receive the average rainfall. While it is not yet possible to predict the exact future pattern of rainfall, the statistical probability that the future will contain a certain proportion of drought and wet years is well known. Nevertheless, the droughts always seem to take us by surprise when they inevitably occur.

If there were some pattern in the occurrence of dry years, it would be possible to increase the accuracy of drought predictions. There must be some underlying climatological organizing principle to southern African droughts, since when they occur, they affect all of the Lowveld, including large parts of Mozambique and Zimbabwe. A casual glance at the long-term rainfall record reveals protracted periods of above- and below-average rainfall. It is tempting to call these patterns cycles, except that in the strict mathematical sense, cycles are as regular as clockwork (and are therefore predictable), whereas the observed patterns are much less well behaved. They may just be due completely to chance – the sort of runs of good and bad luck that a gambler has while throwing dice. When sophisticated statistical techniques designed to reveal cycles are applied to the rainfall data, a weak

twenty-year cycle emerges. In other words, wetter-than-average decades should alternate with drier-than-average decades. However, this cycle accounts for only a small part (about one tenth) of the inter-annual variation, and so is of little use for prediction purposes. Wet cycles contain many dry years, and vice versa.

Climatologists have learned a great deal about the way in which the global climate system works during the past two decades. One important finding they have made is that a large part of the variation in rainfall experienced in southern Africa can be linked to a global pattern known as the El Niño-Southern Oscillation

RIGHT: *The tuber of the water lily* (Nymphaea capensis) *makes a starchy, riparian snack for this baboon.* BELOW: *Buffalo herds can sometimes number several hundred individuals, such as this one at the Kanniedood Dam near Shingwedzi.*

(ENSO) phenomenon. A large pool of warm water accumulates in the eastern equatorial Pacific Ocean and distorts the global system of pressure waves, causing a high pressure cell to dominate over the southern African subcontinent during the summer months.

This type of high pressure system is normal between May and September, and is responsible for the dry and sunny winters. In summer it usually moves offshore, allowing low-pressure systems to draw moist oceanic air over the land, causing the rains. It seems likely that the long Lowveld droughts of the 1930s, 1960s and 1980s were triggered by the ENSO phenomenon. In the future we may have up to 12 months of advance warning of such events, by monitoring sea-surface temperatures and pressure systems in the Pacific and Indian Oceans. It is unclear what an organization such as the Kruger Park, the mission of which includes the conservation of natural processes, should do with such foreknowledge. Is drought mortality a natural process that deserves to be conserved?

Every prolonged drought since the 1930s has resulted in great media concern and campaigns to provide water for the animals. Dams are built and boreholes sunk until the crisis passes. There is little pause to consider the logic and consequences of this water provision.

The irony is that during droughts, wildlife dies mainly of hunger rather than thirst, so providing water does not address the underlying problem, and may even make it worse. Indigenous herbivores obtain most of their water from the food they eat: not from juicy green leaves or dew as is often supposed, but from the chemical reaction that occurs when carbohydrates are broken down, resulting in the release of carbon dioxide and water. Wild animals also control their water loss using a variety of behavioural and physiological adaptations. Their urine, for instance, is highly concentrated, and their faecal pellets are almost dry. Herbivores are most active during early morning and late afternoon, spending the heat of the day resting in the shade.

LEFT: *The haunting call of the African Fish Eagle is for many the evocation of Africa. Television documentaries have made its fishing style familiar to millions of people. It is generally seen perched on a riverbank tree, watching for prey.*

LEFT: *Roan antelope, unkindly nicknamed 'donkeys with horns', are animals specialized for the infertile savannas of Africa. They have had a chequered history in the Kruger National Park: once fairly common in the Pretoriuskop area, their numbers are currently declining. The main population is now found in the northern part of the Park, feeding on the drainage-line grasslands. Roan antelope are apparently reluctant to share water holes with other game.*
BELOW: *An interesting combination of form and function: the Giant Eagle Owl in this picture – which was taken on the Shingwedzi River – is nesting on an abandoned Hamerkop nest in a sycamore fig tree.*

Most of the herbivores in the Kruger Park are concentrated within six kilometres of surface water. This defines the natural limit of the trade-off between the need to obtain food and the need to return to the water-point occasionally for a drink. In the days before boreholes and drinking troughs were provided between the rivers, water dependence was one of the main factors placing a ceiling on game numbers in the Lowveld. The area between the Sand and the Olifants, and the Letaba and Limpopo rivers had no dependable water during the dry season. During the summer, many thousands of small pans were filled with rainwater, and even minor drainage lines had running streams. The herbivores ventured onto the plains only during

Waterbuck

*As the name suggests, waterbuck are always found in close association with water. The white ring around the rump, the shaggy coat and the forward-swept horns of the males are all very distinctive features. The same species (*Kobus ellipsiprymnus*) is found in East Africa but lacks the white rump ring. You may detect the presence of waterbuck even when they are concealed from view by their musky smell. This odour also taints the meat, which is unsuitable as venison.*

Waterbuck favour the green grass and sedges that grow near rivers and are the first herbivores to suffer during periods of prolonged drought. Their social organization is divided into bachelor herds and breeding herds consisting of a dominant male and six to 12 females with calves. The territorial fights among males often lead to serious injuries.

OPPOSITE: *There are literally thousands of temporary water holes (called 'pans') in the Kruger Park. They typically form over the impervious clays of duplex soils found in shallow valleys, and may hold water for a period of a few days to several months.*
FAR RIGHT: *The brightly coloured Malachite Kingfisher is often seen near open water such as dams. It is so small that it can even use grass stems as perches.*

the summer months. This seasonal migration reduced the grazing pressure around the permanent water and imparted some flexibility to the ecosystem during drought years. In times of stress animals could expand their feeding radius slightly to draw on the forage reserves outside their six-kilometre area.

When permanent water is provided in formerly waterless areas the number of animals rapidly increases to the limit that can be carried by the forage growing within the feeding radius around the new water-point. However, now instead of having, say, one thousand hungry animals, there are two thousand hungry animals. Provision of food would be equally counterproductive in the long term, as well as contrary to the objectives of the Park. It would also be prohibitively expensive.

Instead of being partly water-limited, the herbivores are now fully food-limited and are completely at the mercy of the fluctuations in food supply. The result is catastrophic collapses of the inflated herbivore populations, such as occurred in 1966 and again in 1983. Carnivores and scavengers do well for a year, and then their populations also collapse as their prey disappears.

If such events affected only animals, little permanent damage would result. The populations

Foam-Nest Frog

The foam-nest frog is often found in the restcamp bungalows. It is a harmless insect eater with a chameleon-like ability to change colour. Mating is a collaborative effort often involving several pairs. Eggs are laid on a branch overhanging a temporary pan, and the frogs whip the slimy mucous around the eggs into a frothy meringue. The outside of the foam hardens slightly, allowing the tadpoles to develop in the moist interior. After a few days the tadpoles accumulate at the bottom of the foam nest, which ruptures and drops them into the pool below[22].

would breed up again in a few years, ready for another cycle. However, in the process, the vegetation, especially around the water-points, is very heavily eaten. As a result, the grass cover decreases, the perennial species disappear and the trees are stripped and thinned out. When the first heavy rains return, the exposed soil is consequently easily eroded. These processes reduce the capacity of the ecosystem to produce palatable forage in the future. As such, successive episodes of overgrazing put the ecosystem into a vicious downward spiral towards permanent degradation[29].

Another frequently observed consequence of repeated population crashes is that the herbivore community composition changes. The tendency is for formerly diverse herbivore communities, comprising many species in almost equal proportions, to become increasingly dominated by impalas and elephants. Part of the success of elephants is due to the fact that they are able to survive the drought by moving great distances and consuming low-quality forage. Impalas, however, are one of the species encouraged by water provision. Many thousands of impalas die of starvation during the drought period but their high reproductive rate allows their population to recover faster than other species.

Hippos are found only in association with permanent water but are also subject to drought starvation, since aquatic plants form only a minor part of their diet. Most of their grazing takes place on land, especially on the close-cropped lawns they create on the rich alluvial soils alongside rivers. When they are hungry they have been known to wander up to 20 kilometres from the river.

For some reason hippos have a very benign public image, a sort of comic-strip character of plump good-naturedness. The reality is that they can be very dangerous. Males aggressively defend the part of the river which forms their territory. When disturbed hippos head directly for the deepest part of the river – it is best not to be between them and their destination.

Crocodiles are usually found sharing the same waterbodies but their relationship with hippos is uneasy at best. Both hippos and elephants have been known to trample crocodiles. The reason for such behaviour is unknown, since it seems unlikely that crocodiles could regularly harm either species.

OPPOSITE, BELOW: *The African Jacana is a wading bird. It has very long toes which enable it to walk on aquatic vegetation.*
BELOW: *The Saddlebilled Stork is a strikingly distinctive bird generally seen wading through weed-covered waters along the edges of dams, pans or rivers. It is highly dependent on Lowveld rivers for its survival in South Africa. The birds appear to mate for life.*

To understand the present pattern of rivers in the Lowveld, three things need to be considered: climate, geology and geomorphological history. The climate determines the amount of water in the river and therefore its flow characteristics. The last time the Lowveld was a very wet environment, with huge rivers and vast sedimentary deposits, was when the Ecca shales were laid down about 250 million years ago, trapping the vegetation and forming coal deposits in various places in the Park.

The underlying geology has a great influence on the drainage pattern that develops above it. On granites, there is a fine network of small valleys, giving these landscapes

The Rain Tree

Lonchocarpus capassa has several common names, including 'rain tree' and 'appelblaar', which is Afrikaans for 'apple leaf'. The name rain tree has two possible origins: a light breeze through the dry leaves makes a noise that sounds like the patter of raindrops; the tree is also often infested with sap-sucking insects which deliver a steady rain of excreted fluid. Several other Lowveld trees, such as the weeping boer bean (Schotia brachypetala), are also host to these insects.

The rain tree belongs to the subfamily Papilionoideae of the family Fabaceae (also called the Leguminosae, the legume family). The Papilionoideae have distinctive, pea-like flowers which are very showy. The rain tree is no exception – it bears sprays of attractive lilac flowers.

The rain tree is a phreatophyte – that is, its roots reach down to the water table, which may be twenty or more metres below the surface. This enables it to support green leaves during the dry season. Away from rivers, this deep water can usually be reached only via faults and dykes in the bedrock. Rain trees can be seen growing in grooves and lines indicating where these features occur. The association between rain trees and underground water was used as a guide to the location of boreholes before geophysical survey techniques were available.

OPPOSITE, ABOVE: *A water monitor or leguaan scavenging on catfish.* OPPOSITE, BELOW LEFT: *African Fish Eagle.* OPPOSITE, BELOW RIGHT: *Impalas enter water with great care: they have a justifiable fear of crocodiles. Take a moment to marvel at the design of these graceful animals.*

a quilted look from the air. The flat basaltic landscapes have few drainage lines, and the porous sandveld has even fewer. On the hard rhyolite, the rivers are forced to follow the lines of relative weakness provided by dykes of dolerite and therefore flow in parallel straight lines[34].

All the rivers in the Lowveld are incised. This means that they cut rapidly downwards into their channels when the level of the land rose relative to the level of the sea. All the rivers also slice their way through the hard rock of the Lebombo hills. This suggests that they once

OPPOSITE: *White Rhino.* LEFT: *Hamerkop.* BELOW: *Temporary pans dry up very rapidly, sometimes trapping unwary animals in the cloying mud. Warthog, elephant and other relatively hairless animals wallow in the mud in order to rid themselves of ticks. When the mud-pack flakes off the parasites are carried off with it.*

flowed above the hills. Indeed, the tops of the Lebombos show evidence of a surface which existed at this level some five million or more years ago, complete with the rounded pebbles that are characteristic of river beds.

Incised rivers do not have broad flood plains: the valleys of all the Lowveld rivers except the Limpopo are relatively narrow. The river bed is rocky and the banks are steep. The shape of the river valleys permits only a narrow fringe of riparian forest on either bank. The stream spreads out where hard bedrock causes it to

form a braided channel. These rocky expanses are regularly swept by floods and they provide hardly a toehold for plants. The vegetation is therefore permanently in an early stage of succession – consisting of pioneer trees such as the matumi (*Breonadia salicina*) and the waterberry (*Syzigium cordatum*). Upstream of these impediments, the river bed is broad and placid, allowing the deposition of sandbars. These upper reaches typically support reed beds (*Phragmites* species), which provide nest sites for many birds and favoured habitat for buffalo.

The ecology of temporary water holes is fascinating, since the organisms that depend on them must complete their lifecycles in a short and very uncertain period. The Cape terrapin is characteristic of temporary pans: it can often be seen in the tiniest of muddy puddles. The terrapin is perfectly at home on land, which allows it to move between water holes, but is also able to aestivate (a type of suspended animation) in the mud of a dry water hole for many months.

When the pans are full of water, the night-time cacophony of frog calls can be deafening. Some of the most raucous calls are emitted by numerous puddle frogs. A few days after the pans fill, great gelatinous masses of frog spawn appear in them, followed a few days later by masses of tadpoles.

There is something almost mystical about a spring of fresh water in a parched landscape. Springs arise where the water table intersects with the ground surface. Generally, the water table in the Lowveld is many metres below the ground surface, so springs are rare and occur only where a deep valley cuts into the aquifer, or some underground feature forces the water table to the surface. This can sometimes occur along a dyke or fault, or may be caused by an impervious layer that creates a perched water table (a water table above the true water table). Often the water which flows from the spring disappears a few hundred metres further on, as it soaks back into the ground. For a hot spring to exist, the water has to come into contact with the heated rocks deep within the earth's crust. This is possible only where there are faults that penetrate to great depth, such as in the northern part of the Park, where several hot springs occur. The best known are the Matiyovila and Tshalungwa springs, which produce water just warmer than body temperature.

Riparian Restcamps

Both Skukuza and Lower Sabie camps are located on the perennial Sabie River. The Olifants River is in a deeper valley with little forest and is overlooked by Olifants Camp and the Balule Campsite. The Letaba River is broad and sandy at Letaba Camp, and frequently restricted to a series of pools, but there is always water in the Engelhardt Dam, a few kilometres downstream. Shingwedzi Camp is on the river of the same name; Bateleur Camp is also on this river. Malelane Private Camp and Crocodile Bridge Camp are both on the Crocodile River, which has private farms on its southern bank.

Other camps located on smaller watercourses which are dry for part of the year have a charm of their own: Maroela Campsite and Roodewal Private Camp on the Timbavati River; Talamati Bushveld Camp on the N'waswitsonto River; and Jock of the Bushveld Private Camp and Biyamiti Bushveld Camp on the Biyamiti River.

The Best Water holes

The following water-points are those with features that warrant special mention. Klopperfontein, north of Punda Maria, is a fine example of a natural spring. Red Rocks is an attractive spot on the Shingwedzi River where it crosses a band of sandstone and forms a series of potholes, where gold was once panned by 'Texas Jack' Lusk. Mooiplaas on the Tsende River is a good example of the marshy drainage lines that form in flat landscapes located on basalt. The Timbavati River is a classic Lowveld non-perennial river, which can be viewed from the Timbavati Picnic Site or from one of several overlooks. Orpen Dam is in a narrow, rocky valley in the Lebombo hills, with a comfortable hide. Leeupan between Tshokwane and Skukuza is a good example of an open pan, formerly seasonal but now supplied with water. Sunset Dam outside Lower Sabie is a firm favourite of waterbird lovers.

RIGHT: *The Cape (hingeless) terrapins in Kruger live in ephemeral pans, serrated-hinged terrapins (illustrated here) in perennial rivers, and panhinged terrapins are found only in Nyande sandveld pans.*

MOPANEVELD

THE LANDSCAPE NORTH OF THE OLIFANTS RIVER

Mopane trees dominate this region: a grey-green endlessness of horizon-bending flatness and gently swelling relief.

The mopane tree *(Colophospermum mopane)* is a member of the Subfamily Ceasalpinioideae, a group of leguminous trees that dominate the infertile, moist savannas of southern Africa – yet is itself found on arid, relatively fertile soils. Unlike the usual tree cover of arid, fertile soils, the mopane has no thorns but large leaves. Vegetation dominated by mopane trees is known as mopaneveld. There are three main types in the Kruger Park, and they relate to the underlying geology. The western half of the mopaneveld is underlaid with granite-like rocks, which weather to form catenas similar to those described in the Chains of Life chapter which begins on page 56. The coarse, sandy soils at the tops of the ridges are covered with the red bushwillow *(Combretum apiculatum)*, and the mopane occupies the duplex clayey soils of the valley floors. The grasses in granite-based mopaneveld are moderately palatable, but sparse and rather fibrous, so the total game density is low.

ABOVE: *An elephant feeding in dense mopane.* LEFT: *The Cape Glossy Starling will feed on fruit as well as invertebrates, such as harvester termites and flying ants.* OPPOSITE: *Impala grooming in the shade of a mopane tree.*

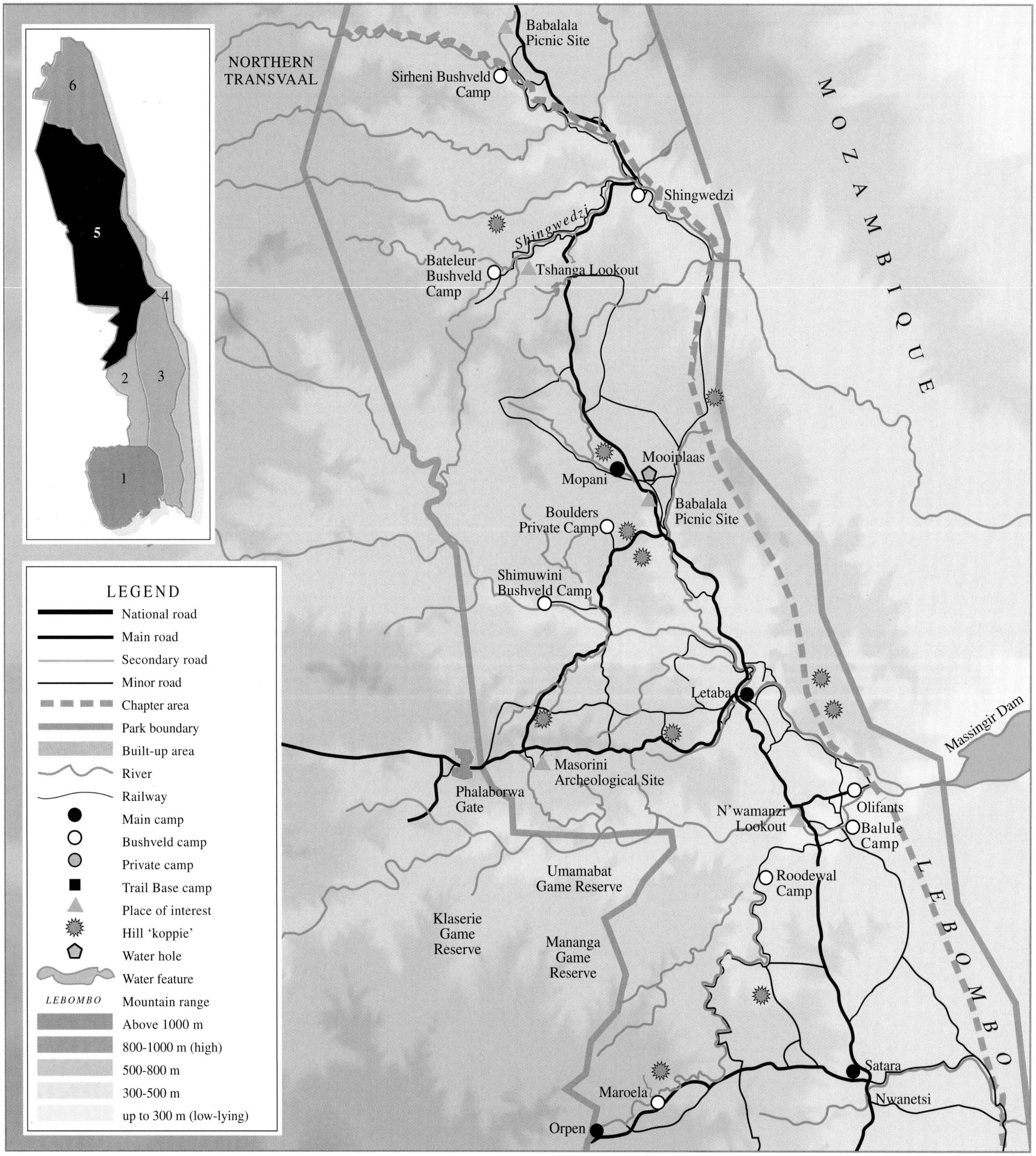
NORTHERN TRANSVAAL
MOZAMBIQUE
LEBOMBO
Babalala Picnic Site
Sirheni Bushveld Camp
Shingwedzi
Shingwedzi
Bateleur Bushveld Camp
Tshanga Lookout
Mooiplaas
Mopani
Babalala Picnic Site
Boulders Private Camp
Shimuwini Bushveld Camp
Letaba
Massingir Dam
Phalaborwa Gate
Masorini Archeological Site
N'wamanzi Lookout
Olifants
Balule Camp
Roodewal Camp
Umamabat Game Reserve
Klaserie Game Reserve
Mananga Game Reserve
Satara
Nwanetsi
Maroela
Orpen
6
5
4
3
2
1
LEGEND
National road
Main road
Secondary road
Minor road
Chapter area
Park boundary
Built-up area
River
Railway
Main camp
Bushveld camp
Private camp
Trail Base camp
Place of interest
Hill 'koppie'
Water hole
Water feature
LEBOMBO
Mountain range
Above 1000 m
800-1000 m (high)
500-800 m
300-500 m
up to 300 m (low-lying)

The eastern half of the mopaneveld is completely different, occurring on basalt that weathers to form a soil called a vertisol (also locally known as turfveld). The mopane trees growing on vertisols are mostly short and the grasses in between are highly palatable and nutritious.

The northern tip of the mopaneveld extends onto Ecca shales, which support stands of tall mopane woodland. In many places the soils on which the mopane grows have a hardened layer at a depth of less than half a metre below the surface. In the western section this is usually due to a deflocculated clay layer, caused by an excess of sodium salts. In the east the hardened layer is usually calcrete, a deposit of lime which occurs in calcium-rich soils where the potential evaporation is much greater than the rainfall. Soluble salts to move upwards in the soil, rather than downwards as they would in wetter climates, and are deposited in hard concretions. This layer acts as a barrier to roots, greatly reducing the effective depth of the soil. Most plants struggle to survive in these soils but mopane thrives.

One does not have to be a botanist to notice that mopane plants come in two forms: a tree, up to ten metres tall with one or more main stems; and a shrub, about three metres tall with many stems. The shrub form can be induced to become a tree by changing its environment, and vice versa. This sort of environmentally induced variation is known as an ecotype.

Even in an extensive stand of shrub mopane, there are always a few individuals that manage to grow into trees. These maintain green leaves during the dry season, long after the other mopane shrubs have dropped theirs. This indicates that they have access to a source of water not generally available.

ABOVE: *The large, paired mopane leaflets are unmistakable, shaped as they are like the wings of a butterfly or the foot-print of an antelope. In the dry season, the leaves of these trees turn a beautiful golden-brown before they fall.*

Following the disturbance of a mopane woodland, for instance by elephants pushing over the mature trees, a large number of competing mopane stems spring up. Some may be seedlings, but most are suckers sprouting from the stem base and roots of the damaged trees. This capacity for vegetative reproduction was originally probably an adaptation to fire but it is also very useful in an environment with frequent physical disturbance. The mopane tree behaves rather like a grass; it simply regrows after being eaten down to the ground.

However, following a disturbance there are so many stems per area of ground that competition between them causes them all to become stuck in the shrubby state. The gradual thinning of the stems occurs naturally given enough time, but there is seldom time for a tall mopane woodland to develop before the next disturbance: the emerging taller trees are pushed over by elephants again, restarting the cycle.

It should be remembered that the elephants do not kill the trees. Rather, they transform them from tree to shrub form. Keeping the vegetation in this state is beneficial to elephants. The low-growing shrubs offer more available browse within their feeding zone.

The gnat-like insects that annoy visitors to the mopaneveld are mopane bees: tiny, stingless cousins of the honey bee. They are social insects that nest in the hollows of mopane trees and produce small amounts of a very sweet honey, prized by San people. Their social organization differs slightly from that of the honey bee, in that the colony contains males as well as females, and the former help with the task of nest-building. The dominance by the queen is also less complete: she has several princesses to assist her with egg laying.

More than half the elephants in the Park live in the mopaneveld. When Stevenson-Hamilton arrived in the Lowveld at the turn of the century, elephants were believed to be locally extinct. The once-plentiful elephant population had been eliminated by ivory hunters.

In 1905 the tell-tale signs of elephant feeding were noted – about twenty elephants were hidden in an inaccessible gorge in the Lebombo hills. Their numbers grew rapidly once the herd was protected in the Park. In fact, the growth was too rapid to be due to reproduction of the local animals alone. Much of the initial increase must have been due to immigration of elephants from Mozambique and Zimbabwe. Since elephants usually bear only one calf at a time, and the period between conception and weaning is nearly three years, the maximum growth rate of an elephant herd is six per cent per annum. The elephant populations of the Kruger Park continue to reproduce at this rate, indicating that they have not yet approached their ecological carrying capacity. Why then are 300 to 600 elephants culled each year in order to stabilize the population at 7 000 animals?

There is theoretical evidence that the long lifespan of the elephants, when coupled with the long life and slow growth of the trees, leads to a system known as a stable limit cycle. This means that the elephant population does not simply rise smoothly to carrying capacity and then level off. The elephant numbers overshoot the carrying capacity, causing the tree population to collapse. The elephants die or move away to a more favourable habitat, causing the local population of elephants to drop below the carrying capacity. Several decades later the trees recover and the elephant population rises again. In theory, therefore, the elephant and tree populations oscillate endlessly around some nominal carrying capacity. Is there any area in Africa that is still large enough to support such a system?

At carrying capacity, animals are living at the limit of their resources. Their condition is poor, and the effects of their feeding on the vegetation are very obvious.

The Park management faces a difficult choice: should they leave the elephant population alone, or should they try to control it? The consequences of leaving it alone would be that many elephants would die naturally and the landscape (especially the trees) would be highly transformed, in a way that disfavours many other species and which most tourists find disturbing. The Park management has chosen to cull elephant. The income derived from the sale of elephant products has little influence on the decision (the culling expenses consume most of the income), nor is it determined by the personal preferences of the management staff, who profoundly dislike the thankless and unpleasant task of killing elephants. After all, most of them became conservationists because

RIGHT: *The oft-repeated story of how the Honeyguide leads the honey badger (also known as the ratel) to the hives of bees is believed to be incorrect – the main target of the Honeyguide's attentions are human. The Honeyguide calls persistently in order to attract attention to itself. Once this has been accomplished, the bird leads its client to a beehive. It is, of course, part of the bargain that the human helping himself to honey then leaves some for the bird. Illustrated here is the Greater Honeyguide.*

ABOVE: *A baboon nibbling scale insects off mopane leaves.* RIGHT: *The fallen leaves form a key part of the diet of many grazers and browsers during the dry season; cattle farmers in mopaneveld call them 'bush biscuits'.*

they love animals. The decision to cull is based on the opinion of experts; the Kruger Park's elephant experts are as good as any, and better than most. Opponents of elephant culling raise two main ecological arguments against the practice: why only elephants and why did the ecosystem not degrade in the distant past, when culling did not occur? The responses to these questions both have to do with spatial scale. By enclosing the Park and altering the surrounding habitat we have weakened processes which operate at large scales, for instance stable limit cycles. These large-scale processes have their greatest effect on large animals such as elephants.

BELOW: *Young bull elephants will often trumpet and raise dust if they feel threatened; female elephants with young can be extremely dangerous and you should keep your distance from them. A relaxed elephant will continue to feed while you watch it.* FAR RIGHT: *Bateleurs are a species of eagle, but during their juvenile phase live mostly on carrion.*

Spatial considerations are the main ecological reason for the removal of the fences between the Kruger National Park and the surrounding wildlife areas. This has already happened along sections of the western boundary, increasing the area of the unbounded ecosystem by some 20 per cent. It is proposed to create a transnational wildlife area on the eastern boundary as well. This will link conservation areas in Zimbabwe, Mozambique and South Africa, and would increase the unfenced area two- to five-fold, creating one of the largest, continuous conserved areas in the world.

Culling elephants raises some particular problems, due to the large size of the animals and their tight social structure. Experience has shown that culling individuals out of a group is disturbing to the remainder of the herd. Therefore, the current practice is to cull entire herds. This has the demographic advantage of not skewing the age and sex ratios in the population.

A herd is located using a helicopter and every member is darted with the immobilizing drug Scoline. It takes about ten minutes to dart an entire herd containing ten to twenty animals. As soon as the drugged animals present a stationary target, they are shot in the brain from the helicopter. This is the cause of death; the Scoline is used simply to avoid wounding the animals due to inaccurate shots aimed at a moving target. A team of rangers on the ground ensures that the elephants are dead if there is any doubt. The carcasses are transported to a facility near Skukuza, where they are processed into canned and dried meat and salted hides.

In recent years, young elephants have sometimes been captured instead of culled, for transport to other conserved areas, but this practice has not been without problems. When the young animals are released into their new habitat, they are without the support of the family social unit. Not only do they struggle to learn which plants to eat and which to avoid, they behave in a reclusive way and they can be dangerous to humans.

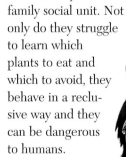

CITES, the Convention on the International Trade in Endangered Species, bans international trade in ivory. South Africa is a signatory to this treaty, but it has consistently voted

and argued against this provision, on the basis that the commercial exploitation of non-threatened wildlife populations is the best way to ensure their conservation.

Despite not being legally required to do so, South Africa nevertheless observes the international trade ban on ivory, so most of the tusks resulting from elephant culling in the Kruger Park are simply stored. A small quantity has in the past been used to produce ivory articles for sale within South Africa.

ABOVE: *Leopards are the most widespread and adaptable of all the large cats – they can be found from the icy mountain tops to the hot desert fringes. These animals do, however, show a preference for areas with trees.*
RIGHT: *The Arrowmarked Babbler travels in gregarious, noisy flocks. It eats mainly insects, and also small vertebrates, which it finds by searching about in leaf-litter.*
OPPOSITE, TOP RIGHT: *Tall mopane trees.*

MOPANE WORM

There are several organisms that base their entire lifecycle around the mopane tree. The mopane worm is the larva of a type of emperor moth, and feeds exclusively on mopane leaves. Like many leaf-eating worms, its population dynamics are characterized by massive outbreaks, separated by several years during which the worm is hard to find. During an outbreak, hectares of the trees are defoliated. This does the trees little harm. The worm is a highly valued protein source among indigenous African people. Large numbers of the larvae are collected and cooked, or dried for future use.

African countries are divided (approximately north and south of the Zambezi River) on the issue of the ivory trade. The East African countries, supported by Europe and America, argue that it is necessary to suspend the trade in legal ivory in order to destroy the powerful and well-armed syndicates that control the illegal trade. Attempts to control trade on the supply side by anti-poaching measures have failed. The alternative is to destroy the demand for ivory in the consumer countries, which are mostly in Asia.

The southern African nations argue that the African elephant is not an endangered species, especially in their region, where effective conservation measures have seen the populations increase to levels where they are causing damage to crops and the habitat of other species. Preventing the trade in ivory goods makes it uneconomical to cull these animals in countries where the wildlife management sector is less well funded than in South Africa. It also undermines the efforts of conservation authorities to make wildlife a beneficial resource to poverty-stricken rural populations; innovative schemes which make wildlife the economic mainstay for developing communities are dependent on the income from valuable species such as elephant.

Rhinos definitely are endangered species: the global population of black rhino is under 3 000, and falling fast. The cause of the decline is the poaching of these animals for their valuable horns. Ivory is used mainly for jewellery and carved objects by a relatively small, wealthy and

literate clientele, who may be persuaded not to buy elephant products. Rhino horn, however, is used as a traditional medicine by many poorer Asians and for ornamental dagger-handles in the Middle East. These markets are less easily influenced. Since the small quantities of horn are easily smuggled, demand-side control is extremely difficult. There are thus few short-term alternatives to aggressive anti-poaching operations.

The translocation of animals into areas where they can be protected, and the removal of their horns (which regrow in about three years), have been undertaken in a desperate attempt to save the species, but these procedures are costly, and detrimental to the populations themselves. The long-term solutions must be based on education of the horn-users about the impact they are having on the animals. Without a reduction in demand, it will never be possible to reach a

OPPOSITE AND RIGHT: *Young spotted hyaena romping and play-fighting in a bed of autumnal mopane leaves. Hyaenas live in clans of eight to 12 animals, and these occupy a territory of about 25 square kilometres. The call is part of the territorial marking behaviour that includes scent-marking from the anal glands.*
OPPOSITE, BELOW: *Whitebacked Vulture.*

situation where the demand can be sustainably met by the supply. The Kruger Park has recorded several cases of rhino and elephant poaching in recent years but is relatively fortunate in this regard in comparison to other African wildlife areas. This is due partly to the existence of well-trained and vigilant Park staff.

The large die-offs of hippos during each drought suggests that their population in the Kruger Park is probably close to its carrying capacity. Hippo culling is justified by the Park management largely in terms of the dwindling water supply in Lowveld rivers and the consequent reduction in hippo habitat.

The ecological reasons for culling buffalo are based on the argument that if they are allowed to reach carrying capacity, they will so alter the nature of the grassland that other, rarer species such as roan will be detrimentally affected. Buffalo, like the cattle they resemble, are capable of overgrazing the grassland if continuously present in high numbers. The tall grass of the 'climax' grassland would give way to shorter, sparser 'subclimax' grasses, encouraging a different spectrum of grazers. These arguments are largely untested; since buffalo are one of the favoured prey of lions, there is some reason to hope that the buffalo population might be naturally regulated if given the chance. Another reason for culling buffalo is veterinary – buffalo harbour many diseases which can be transmitted to cattle. On the other hand, these same diseases should help to control the buffalo populations without outside interference. The number of buffalo culled in the Kruger Park varies considerably from year to year, but is often several thousand.

The tsessebe population of the Park is currently concentrated on the basaltic grasslands and mopaneveld in the northeast, although Stevenson-Hamilton recorded them as being relatively common around Pretoriuskop earlier

ABOVE, LEFT: *The Kruger National Park is the southern limit of the sable antelope's distribution.* ABOVE, RIGHT: *Lion hunting from the cover of a shrub mopane.* RIGHT: *Mopane worms are eagerly eaten by birds such as hornbills which are large enough to cope with a slightly spiny worm as long and thick as your thumb. Here a Redbilled Hornbill forages for insects on the trunk of an old mopane.*
OPPOSITE, RIGHT: *More than half the elephants found in Kruger live in the mopaneveld. This herd was photographed near Shingwedzi.*

CIVET

Civets, like genets, are small, cat-like predators that belong to the mongoose family (Viveridae). They are often seen scavenging in restcamps at night. Although they can become quite tame, they should not be fed or touched because they will bite and can harbour diseases transmissible to humans, such as tetanus or rabies. This precaution applies to all wild animals.

Male and female civets both weigh about ten kilograms at maturity. Their diet consists of insects, mice, fruit, small birds and reptiles, and a small amount of green grass.

Civets defecate in latrines, which may be used by a number of individuals. They mark their territories with a secretion of the perineal gland. This secretion has a remarkable ability to retain its smell and was once used as a fixative by the perfume industry.

in the century. Tsessebe bulls are highly territorial, and can often be seen standing on one of their territorial markers, such as a termite mound or dung-heap. The breeding herd, which consists entirely of cows and juvenile animals, remains exclusively within the male territory. Subadult males are chased out of the herd when they are one year old, and form bachelor herds outside the territory. The tsessebe is reputed to be the fastest antelope. The young are able to keep up with their mothers within hours of being born – an attribute essential for survival on the open plains.

The shy bat-eared fox is a desert animal and rare in the Park. It was first recorded in 1967 near Shingwedzi and appears to have arrived from the Kalahari in the west or the arid sandveld to the east, via the dry corridor offered by

TOP, LEFT: *Crested Barbets nest in neat, round holes which they bore into tree trunks.*
ABOVE, LEFT: *A lioness in the glow of the late afternoon sun.*
OPPOSITE: *Every wild dog has a unique coat pattern, and biologists studying wild dog populations have used photographs taken by visitors to estimate the number of wild dogs in the Park.*

the Limpopo Valley. Bat-eared foxes are confined to the mopaneveld and grasslands in the north of the Kruger National Park.

The mopaneveld has historically been the least-visited part of the Park. Many regard it as the Park's best-kept secret. However, with the building of several new camps (Mopani, and the smaller camps at Boulders, Shimuwini and Bateleur) the secret seems to be out.

Tourist Facilities in the Mopaneveld

There are four full-facility restcamps in the mopaneveld region: Olifants, Letaba, Mopani and Shingwedzi. Olifants and Mopani have no camping or caravanning facilities but there is a campsite at Balule, ten kilometres south of Olifants. Olifants Camp (264 beds) is justifiably famous for its magnificent setting, overlooking the top of the Olifants River Gorge, where it begins to cleave its way through the Lebombo range. Letaba Camp is located on the river of the same name, which is broad, sandy and often dry. It is a firm favourite with regular Park visitors because of its restful, shady atmosphere (355 beds and 240 campsites). The Automobile Association office for the northern part of the Park is located there. Shingwedzi (270 beds and

BELOW, LEFT: *Wahlberg's Eagle is possibly the most common eagle in Africa. Unlike any other eagle in southern Africa, it is a breeding migrant to the region, arriving at the start of summer and leaving again in March.*
RIGHT: *Baobab trees in the northern part of the Park are a good place to look for the swift-like birds known as Spinetails, which nest in them. There are two species, Böhm's and Mottled, which are both rare in South Africa.*

330 campsites) is one of the oldest camps in the Park. If you are visiting the north of the Park in the summer months this is a good choice, since it has a large swimming pool. Mopani Camp (506 beds), newest of the four, also has a swimming pool and is the only northern camp with conference facilities. Boulders is a private camp and accommodates 12. Shimuwini (71 beds in all), Bateleur (34 beds) and Sirheni (80 beds) are small bushveld camps, offering fewer facilities than the main camps (no restaurants or shops) but a more private atmosphere. The accommodation is in two- or three-bedroom cottages sleeping four to six people each.

You may get out of your vehicle to stretch your legs at Tshanga (where there are toilets), N'wamanzi and at the bird hide outside Shingwedzi. There are full picnic facilities at Masorini, Babalala and Mooiplaas. In addition to picnic facilities, Masorini also has an interesting archaeological display and reconstruction of the iron-working village that used to exist there in pre-colonial times.

THE LAST FRONTIER

THE LANDSCAPE AROUND PUNDA MARIA AND PAFURI

The northern tip of the Kruger Park is at the crossroads of both history and biology. Not only is it the point where the political boundaries of South Africa, Mozambique and Zimbabwe coincide, it also represents the intersection between several important biological regions.

Biogeographers, who study the patterns revealed by the distribution of plants and animals, divide the world up into regions which share similar groups of species. The boundaries of the plant regions do not always coincide with those for animals, since the factors controlling these groups differ. When conservation biologists select locations for protection, they usually do so on the basis of the level of biological diversity which these areas contain. If the northern part of the Kruger Park were not already a conserved area, it would be one of the prime areas in southern Africa in which to create one[30]. The high biodiversity found here is mainly due to the large number of different habitats packed into a small area, which in turn reflect the underlying geology and landscape structure.

The hills on which Punda Maria is located are the eastern extension of the Soutpansberg. They are built of Wyliespoort quartzite, a hard rock which is resistant to weathering[3]. The Soutpansberg is an upthrust block (or graben) between a series of parallel faults which run in an east-west direction. These faults are part

ABOVE: *A pair of Bateleurs.* LEFT: *The Pied Kingfisher can be seen hovering over most stretches of water.* OPPOSITE: *White seringa sunset.*

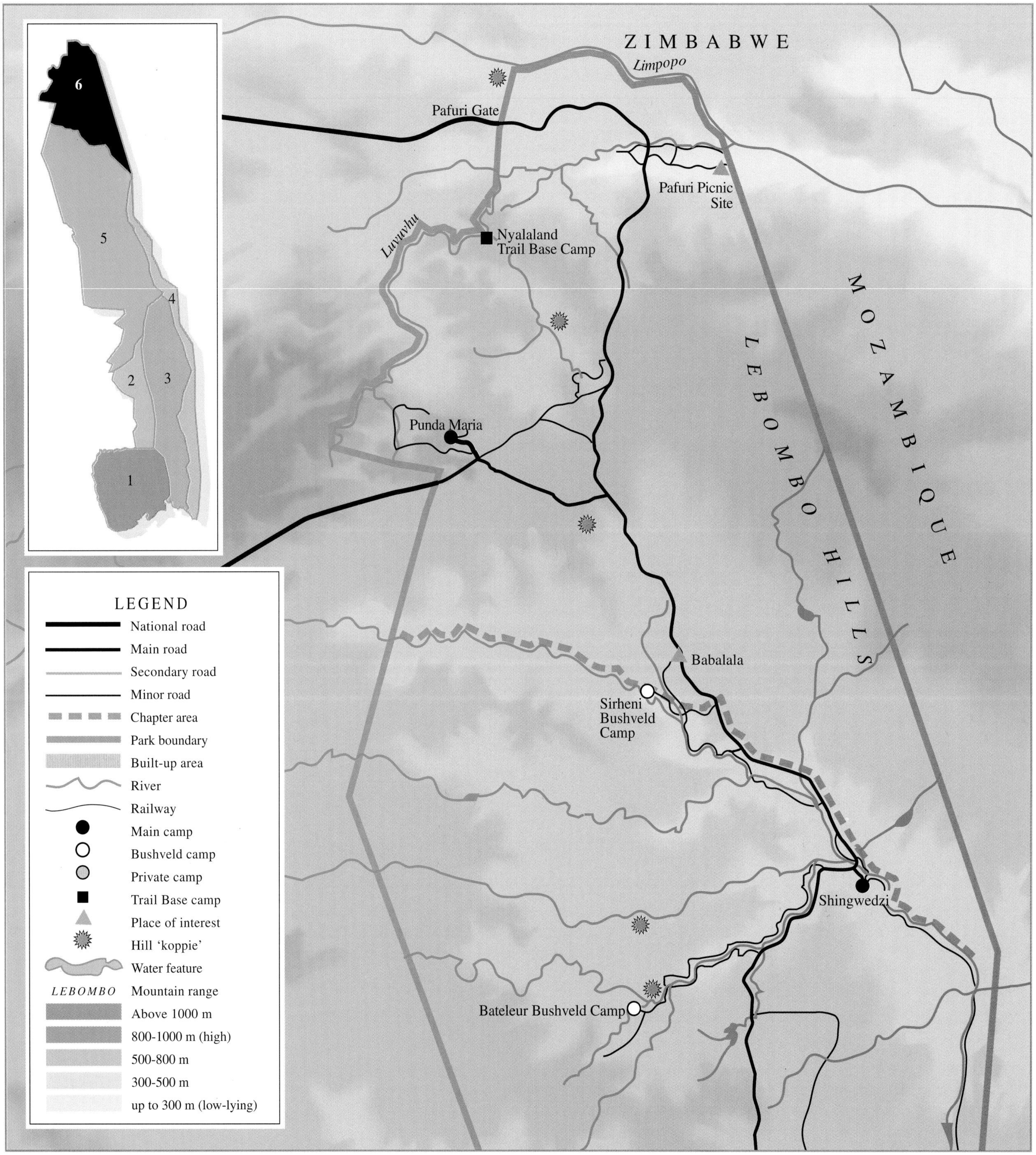
ZIMBABWE
Limpopo
Pafuri Gate
Pafuri Picnic Site
Luvuvhu
Nyalaland Trail Base Camp
MOZAMBIQUE
LEBOMBO HILLS
Punda Maria
Babalala
Sirheni Bushveld Camp
Shingwedzi
Bateleur Bushveld Camp
6
5
4
2
3
1
LEGEND
National road
Main road
Secondary road
Minor road
Chapter area
Park boundary
Built-up area
River
Railway
Main camp
Bushveld camp
Private camp
Trail Base camp
Place of interest
Hill 'koppie'
Water feature
LEBOMBO Mountain range
Above 1000 m
800-1000 m (high)
500-800 m
300-500 m
up to 300 m (low-lying)

ABOVE: *The Green Pigeon is a common fruit-eater in the Lowveld. Listen for its gurgling coo, especially in areas of riparian forest.* RIGHT: *The delicate beauty of the flame lily (*Gloriosa superba*) belies the fact that this plant can kill in four hours if eaten.*

of the Limpopo Mobile Belt, the joint between the piece of crust on which most of South Africa is located (the Kaapvaal Craton) and the Central African Craton to the north. The depth of these faults is indicated by the number of hot springs that occur along them: a fault must penetrate right down to the superheated rock of the lower crust to generate hot water.

The Soutpansberg tilts steeply downwards towards the east. A drop in rainfall accompanies the declining altitude. Pafuri is the driest location in the Park (on average it receives 400 millimetres per annum), but only 100 kilometres to the west is Entabeni which, at 1 900 metres altitude in the Soutpansberg, receives 1 900 millimetres per annum. The Punda Maria hills capture a little additional moisture from fog, indicated by grey-green tufts of lichen or 'old man's beard' (*Usnea* species) hanging from the trees.

The isolated Soutpansberg has a remarkably diverse population of small reptiles. Several of these penetrate into the Kruger Park and are found in the Punda Maria area: for instance, the montane blind skink, the rough-tailed girdled lizard and the tigroid thick-toed gecko.

South of Punda Maria are mopane-covered basaltic plains. East and north of the Soutpansberg quartzites are sediments of the Karoo sequence, as are encountered south of the Olifants River. The Ecca shales, which in the south support a dense *Acacia* thicket, here support tall mopane woodland. This is a good place to look for Arnot's Chat, an endemic mopaneveld bird.

BELOW: *The Longtailed Glossy Starling is one of the special birds of the far northern areas.* RIGHT: *Buffalo photographed on a thundery day near Punda Maria.*

The uppermost stratum in the Karoo sedimentary sequence is Clarens sandstone. This is the relatively hard rock through which the Luvuvhu River cuts the Lanner Gorge, and which gives the landscape much of its character. Clarens sandstone weathers to form steep, pinkish-yellow cliffs and rugged rock outcrops. It is also well known for the cave overhangs which form at the bases of the cliffs, and which were favourite homes of the San people.

This rocky area is also the only habitat in the Park that supports the yellow-spotted rock dassie. It is very similar in appearance to the common rock dassie and differs only in being slightly smaller and having whitish patches above the eyes. Rock dassies are browsers and the bushes close to their communal dens are often stunted by the regular pruning they receive. The dassies venture only about twenty metres from their craggy refuges. This distance is finely gauged to allow them to dash back to safety if they spot a swooping eagle.

After the Luvuvhu River emerges from the rocky gorge that it cuts through the Karoo sediments, its character changes completely. From being a swiftly flowing stream, the river debouches onto a broad flood plain. The silt which is carried by the fast-moving waters is deposited as a rich alluvial plain.

This plain joins with the alluvial fringes of the Limpopo River to form a fascinating, dry riparian forest habitat.

LEFT: *The yellow-green bark of the fever tree (*Acacia xanthophloea*) gives it a sickly appearance, but the origin of the name derives from the observation of early explorers that it was unhealthy to camp in areas where these trees grow.*

The channel of the Luvuvhu River itself is sometimes dry, but the tall trees on either bank are supported by subsurface water. The Pafuri forests are the only place in the Park where samango monkeys are to be found. They were introduced in the 1980s, having been recorded here previously only in exceptionally wet years.

The confluence of the Limpopo and Luvuvhu is famous for its ghostly stands of fever trees (*Acacia xanthophloea*), so named because they

LEFT: *Many of the sycamore fig trees lining the Luvuvhu River died during a severe drought in 1991 and 1992.* BELOW, LEFT: *Elephants once roamed freely across the international borders at 'Crook's Corner', and so did elephant poachers.* BELOW, RIGHT: *Burchell's Coucal or the Rainbird, as it is also known, is a shy species with a lovely, bubbling call.*

grow in swampy ground where mosquitoes, carriers of malaria, are common. Some of these fever tree forests are now dying, apparently due to the lowered water table brought about the reduced flow in the Luvuvhu River; fortunately, new stands are developing north of the river.

The ephemeral pans on the northeastern border of the Kruger Park were the only known location in South Africa of the African lungfish[25], which possesses a true lung instead of gills. This allows it to survive for long periods in 'cocoons' which it forms in the mud of dried-out pans. Specimens have now been translocated to Machanyi Pan southeast of Pafuri, and Rietpan north of Lower Sabie, to make the conservation of this interesting species more secure within South Africa.

The hottest and most arid part of the Park is that north of the Luvuvhu River. As is typical of hot, dry savannas on stony soils, trees are dominated by the genus *Commiphora* (the Afrikaans name, 'kanniedood', means 'cannot be killed'). Commiphoras are identified mostly by their bark: typically papery and peeling – an

NYALA BERRY TREE

The nyala berry tree (Xanthocercis zambeziaca) *is a huge, spreading tree found only where its roots have permanent water. It is a very unusual member of the legume family, since it has a fleshy fruit rather than a pod.*

adaptation possibly to shield the stem from the fierce sun. In some species, a sheet large enough to write a letter on can be peeled off.

One landscape in the north contributes disproportionately to the uniqueness and diversity of the area. It is the large tract of deep, sandy soil where the vegetation is called sandveld. There are smaller patches of similar soil in several places in the Park (notably the Pumbe sandveld in the Lebombos), but nowhere as extensive as it is in the north. The second large block of sandveld lies on the western boundary of the Park, south of Punda Maria northwards to Pafuri. It originates from Karoo system sandstones which themselves formed from wind-blown desert sands, rather like those found in the Kalahari and Nyandu sandveld. This area of sandveld, on the Mahogany Loop west of Punda Maria, is one of the few accessible to tourists.

This area supports tall, broad-leaved woodlands like the miombo woodlands of Central Africa. Because of the infertility of the soils on which they grow, miombo woodlands do not support high densities of wildlife, but they do contain characteristic plants, animals and birds like the Mashona Hyliota.

The sandveld plateau may formerly have represented the southernmost distribution of the normal range of Lichtenstein's hartebeest (although there is evidence that it may have occurred in the southern part of the Park, and even as far south as Lake St Lucia). It became locally extinct at the beginning of this century. In 1985 the Parks Board decided to reintroduce Lichtenstein's hartebeest to the Park. Fifteen animals were captured in Malawi and relocated 25 kilometres south of Punda Maria. In 1986 a further 15 animals were added to the herd, which is now breeding successfully.

Two plants common in tropical Africa but in South Africa confined to the sandveld of the northern Kruger Park are the sand camwood (*Baphia massaiensis*) and the wing pod (*Xeroderris stuhlmannii*), both of which belong to the subfamily Papilionoideae. The Papilionoideae are notable for their attractive flowers

(from which the name, meaning 'butterfly-like', derives) and the nodules on their roots which contain bacteria capable of turning nitrogen from the atmosphere into fertiliser for the plant.

The suni, the smallest antelope in the Park and one of the rarest, is known only from the sandveld thickets in the northern part of the Park. It is a tropical species, more common in northern KwaZulu-Natal and Mozambique.

There is a variety of animals which are predominantly found on deep, sandy soils. The springhare, a rodent with an ancient relationship to hares, needs such soils in which to burrow. It emerges only after sunset, so is seldom seen by tourists. This animal looks like a small kangaroo, with long, powerful hind legs that

BELOW, LEFT: *Doublebanded Sandgrouse will fly vast distances daily to drink. They carry moisture to their chicks in their breast feathers.*
BELOW AND RIGHT: *Nyala were first recorded in the Park in the 1920s.*

ABOVE: *The Crested Guineafowl is a shy, forest species.* BELOW, RIGHT: *The rock hyrax, or dassie, is found on rocky outcrops. It has no close evolutionary relatives apart from the other hyrax species.* OPPOSITE: *The Luvuvhu River's broad strip of riverine forest is home to the rare Pel's Fishing Owl.*

propel it in bounds of up to two metres while it uses its long tail for balance. Despite this it is completely unrelated to the kangaroo. The springhare is highly sought-after by the San people who winkle it out of its two metre-long burrow (complete with escape tunnel) with the aid of a long, flexible stick with a barb at the end. It is estimated that two and a half million springhares are eaten every year in Botswana alone[27].

The Thickbilled Cuckoo and the Racquet-tailed Roller both reach their southern limit in the sandveld of the northern Kruger Park.

There are several very rare reptiles whose first or only records in South Africa are from this location: the white-lipped snake, the blue-tailed sandveld lizard, Leonhard's spade-nosed worm lizard, and Lang's roundheaded worm lizard.

The first ranger in this region, J J Coetzer, named his outpost Punda Maria. The Parks Board renamed it Punda Milia under the impression that he had misspelled the Swahili word for zebra ('punda miliya'). In fact he had intended the name as a pun on that of his wife (Maria) and her predilection for striped dresses. The original spelling has now been restored.

The escape of ranger Harry Wolhuter from the jaws of a lion is a well-known story, but few people have heard of Nombolo Mdluli, who shot the lion that had pinned down ranger Trollope, and later shot another man-eating lion at Shingwedzi. Others were less fortunate: several black rangers have been killed by wild animals or by poachers in the line of duty. Shabangu Mafuta set out alone in pursuit of a pride of lions which had been harassing people at Kemp's Cottage. He shot and wounded a large lioness, but on following it into thick bush it sprang at him and he was able to fire only one shot before having to clamber up a low tree. The wounded lioness dragged him out of the tree and mauled him very badly before he was able to kill it with his pen-knife.

Shabangu Mafuta died from loss of blood, after having dragged himself four hundred metres in the direction of his home.

Much of the work of building the Park infrastructure and protecting its animals has been (and still is) performed by blacks[5]. The Kruger Park has had paid black staff from the earliest days. By 1941 the conservation staff included eight black sergeants and 120 rangers; at the time there were approximately 12 white conservators. Several of the place names in the Kruger Park commemorate these men: Doispane Road after Doispane Mongwe; Shithlave Road is named after Sergeant Jafuta (Masabane) Shithlave, who trained black rangers and whose sense of discipline is still spoken of in awe; and Jan-se-Pan after Sergeant Jan Hatlane of Punda Maria.

Forty years of apartheid disadvantaged black staff in two ways: they were excluded from positions of authority, and the poor educational opportunities prevented them from qualifying for posts requiring technical skills.

The wildlife areas of the Lowveld have, until recently, been a man's world. Women were appointed only in service roles, such as in the tourist camps. Despite the restricted scope that was available to them, principally as rangers' wives, many women have made significant contributions to the success of the Park. Women are still almost completely absent from the ranger ranks although a quarter of those working as research staff are now female.

These legacies are a severe handicap to the effective fulfillment of the Park's mission as it enters a new era in South African history, and they are actively being addressed by the Parks Board. The challenges facing the Park are now mostly political rather than ecological. How can it make itself relevant to the entire population of South Africans and how can it build relationships of mutual benefit and respect with the communities living on the Park borders?

Pre-colonial History

Long before the first white explorers reached this land, there was a well-trodden trade route between the Limpopo Valley and Sofala and Inhambane on the east coast of Africa[20]. The people of the interior traded ivory, gold, copper, tin and slaves with the Arabs, for beads, ceramics,

ABOVE: *The Thulamela archaeological site is being excavated and is documented in a nearby museum.* OPPOSITE, ABOVE RIGHT: *Dr Sydney Miller works with pottery shards from Thulamela.* RIGHT: *Artefacts from the site, dated at between 10 000 and a million years old.* OPPOSITE, BELOW: *Whitefronted Bee-eater.*

cloth and implements. Trade produced the wealth that allowed clans to unite into kingdoms and build cities such as Mapungubwe and Great Zimbabwe, a culture which peaked in the thirteenth century. Its collapse coincided with the capture of the Arab ports on the east coast by the Portuguese in the sixteenth century.

The Venda people, who occupy land around the northern part of the Kruger National Park, are descendants of the builders of the walled cities of the Zimbabwe culture. They are more

Lala Palm

*The lala palm (*Hyphaene coriacea*) is an indication that the soil is wet for part of the year. Lala palms are frequently found in low-lying areas where the soil is poorly drained. The sap of this species is collected by African people to make an alcoholic beverage. One plant will yield several litres of sap over several days. A skilled palm-tapper shaves thin slices from the crown of the plant to keep the sap flowing, without damaging the apical bud.*

*The fronds are used to weave baskets. They are straw-coloured when dried, but are often interwoven with fronds that are dyed brown by boiling them with the roots of the magic gwarri (*Euclea divinorum*). The fruits contain a large white kernel that is known as 'vegetable ivory'.*

closely related to the Shona people of Zimbabwe than to the Nguni, Sotho or Tswana people of South Africa.

The ruins of two large, stone-walled villages have been found overlooking the Luvuvhu River. The village at Thulamela, ten kilometres west of Pafuri, has recently been the site of an archaeological excavation. Articles from the site have been dated to the period 1460-1640, confirming that Thulamela was occupied during the last phase of the Zimbabwe culture, following the fragmentation of the Monomatapa kingdom. The finely crafted stone walling and extent of the site identify it as a royal village. Trade goods and gold wire have been recovered from ongoing excavations at the ruins. A similar stone-walled village is located at Makahane. An archaeological and cultural display is planned for Thulamela, which is one of the most important archaeological sites in the Park.

Tourist Facilities in the Far North of the Park

There is only one tourist camp in this region, Punda Maria. In addition, there is a trails camp called Nyala Land, in the wilderness area south of the Luvuvhu River, and a popular picnic site at Pafuri. The hutted part of Punda Maria Camp is small (48 beds); most of the accommodation is in the form of campsites for 300 visitors. The camp is in a beautiful location on a wooded hillside and preserves a quiet, relaxed atmosphere. The self-guided walking trail within the camp is a good way to see birds and trees which are rare elsewhere in South Africa. For tree-lovers, the Mahogany Loop starts and ends near Punda Maria. It passes through sandveld with species such as *Androstachys johnsonii*, *Burkea africana* and *Kirkia acuminata*, not easily seen elsewhere in the Park. The picnic site at Pafuri is in an idyllic location among the trees of the Luvuvhu flood plain. It offers toilets, shade, tables and chairs, braai facilities and hot water.

The most northerly entrance to the Park is Pafuri Gate, 76 kilometres north of Punda Maria. The Punda Maria Gate is just nine kilometres west of the Punda Maria Restcamp.

REFERENCES

The National Parks Board publishes a bimonthly popular magazine, *Custos*, an annual journal of research, *Koedoe*, and the Annual Report of the Board. All three contain a wealth of information relating to the Kruger Park. Superscript numbers in the text refer to the corresponding numbers of the entries below.

1. Arnold, T.H. and De Wet B.C. 1993. 'Plants of Southern Africa: Names and distribution.' *Memoirs of the Botanical Survey of South Africa* 62. Pretoria: National Botanical Institute.

2. Barton, J.M., Bristow, J.W. and Venter, F.J. 1986. 'A summary of the Precambrian Granitoid Rocks of the Kruger National Park.' *Koedoe* 29, 39-44.

3. Bristow, J.W. 1986. 'An overview of the Soutpansberg sedimentary and volcanic rocks.' *Koedoe* 29, 59-68

4. Bristow, J.W. and Venter, F.J. 1986. 'Notes on the Permian to recent geology of the Kruger National Park.' *Koedoe* 29, 85-104

5. Carruthers, J. 1993. '"Police boys" and poachers: Africans, wildlife protection and national parks, the Transvaal 1902-1950.' *Koedoe* 36, 11-22.

6. Chappel, C.A. and Brown, M.A. 1993. 'The use of remote sensing in quantifying rates of soil erosion.' *Koedoe* 36, 1- 14.

7. Chittenden, H. 1992. *Top birding spots in Southern Africa.* Johannesburg: Southern.

8. Coates Palgrave, K. 1977. *Trees of Southern Africa.* Cape Town: Struik.

9. Fourie, P.F. 1992. *Kruger National Park: Questions and Answers.* Cape Town: Struik.

10. Fraser, S.W., van Rooyen, T.H. and Verster, E. 1987. 'Soil-plant relationships in the Central Kruger National Park.' *Koedoe* 30, 19-34.

11. Gertenbach, W.P.D. 1980. 'Rainfall patterns in the Kruger National Park.' *Koedoe* 23, 35-43.

12. Gertenbach, W.P.D. 1983. 'Landscapes of the Kruger National Park.' *Koedoe* 26, 9-122.

13. Guy, G.L. 1969. '*Adansonia digitata* and its rate of growth in relation to rainfall in South Central Africa.' *Proceedings and Transactions of the Rhodesian Scientific Association* 54, 68-84.

14. Hall-Martin, A.J. 1987. 'Range expansion of the Yellowbilled Oxpecker *Buphagus africanus* into the Kruger National Park, South Africa.' *Koedoe* 30, 121-132.

15. *Kruger National Park 1993: Make the most of Kruger.* Johannesburg: Jacana Education.

16. Mundy, P., Butchart, D., Ledger, J. and Piper, S. 1992. *The vultures of Africa.* Johannesburg: Acorn Books.

17. Pienaar, U. de V. 1969. 'Predator-prey relationships among the larger mammals of the Kruger National Park.' *Koedoe* 12, 108-176.

18. Pienaar, U. de V. 1978. *The freshwater fishes of the Kruger National Park.* Pretoria: National Parks Board.

19. Pienaar, U. de V. 1985. 'Indications of progressive dessication of the Transvaal lowveld over the past 100 years, and implications for the water stabilization programme in the Kruger National Park.' *Koedoe* 28, 93-165.

20. Pienaar, U. de V. 1990. *Neem uit die verlede.* Pretoria: National Parks Board.

21. Pienaar, U. de V., Joubert, S.C.J., Hall-Martin, A., de Graaf, G. and Rautenbach, I.L. 1987. *Field Guide to the Mammals of the Kruger National Park.* Cape Town: Struik.

22. Pienaar, U. de V., Passmore, N.I., and Carruthers, V.C. 1976. *The frogs of the Kruger National Park.* Pretoria: National Parks Board.

23. Pienaar, U. de V, Rautenbach, I.L. and de Graaf, G. 1980. *The Small Mammals of the Kruger National Park.* Pretoria: National Parks Board.

24. Schutte, I.C. 1986. 'The general geology of the Kruger National Park.' *Koedoe* 29, 13-37.

25. Skelton, P. 1993. *A Complete Guide to the Freshwater Fishes of South Africa.* Johannesburg: Southern.

26. Sinclair, I. and Whyte, I. *Field Guide to the Birds of the Kruger National Park.* Cape Town: Struik.

27. Smithers, R.H.N. 1983. *The Mammals of the Southern African Subregion.* Pretoria: University of Pretoria.

28. Stevenson-Hamilton, J. 1937. *South African Eden.* Cape Town: Struik.

29. Thrash, I., Nel, P.J., Theron, G.K. & Bothma, J. du P. 1991. 'The impact of the provision of water for game on the basal cover of the herbaceous vegetation around a dam in the Kruger National Park.' *Koedoe* 34, 121-152.

30. Tinley, K.L. 1980. From the Tinley Report. *African Wildlife*, special issue: 'The fight against coal mining in the Kruger National Park.'

31. Trollope, W.S.W. 1993. 'Fire regime of the Kruger National Park for the period 1980-1992.' *Koedoe* 36, 45-52.

32. Trollope, W.S.W., Potgieter A.L.F. and Zambatis, N. 1989. 'Assessing veld condition in the Kruger National Park using key grass species.' *Koedoe* 32, 67-94.

33. Van Wyk, P. 1972. *Trees of the Kruger National Park.* Volumes 1 and 2. Cape Town: Purnell

34. Venter, F.J. and Bristow, J.W. 1986. 'An account of the geo-morphology of the Kruger National Park.' *Koedoe* 29, 117- 124.

35. Wolhuter, H. 1948. *Memories of a Game Ranger.* Johannesburg: Wildlife Society.

INDEX

Bold *Numbers Refer to Visual Material*